INTRODUCTION TO
USUL AL-FIQH

INTRODUCTION TO
USUL AL-FIQH

BY **FURHAN ZUBAIRI**

Printed in the United States of America

First Publishing, 2019

ISBN: 9781677761937

Content input: Jawad Beg
Cover design, layout, and typesetting: Mohammad Bibi
Typeset in Lato, Nassim, and KFGQPC Uthmanic Script HAFS
Arabic Symbols: KFGQPC Arabic Symbols 01

Dedicated to my parents, family, and teachers.
May Allah continue to bless them and grant them
the highest ranks in Paradise.

CONTENTS

PART 2

Transliteration & Pronunciation Key

Arabic Letter	Transliteration	Sound
ء	ʾ	A slight catch in the breath, cutting slightly short the preceding syllable.
ا	*ā*	An elongated *a* as in *cat.*
ب	*b*	As in *best.*
ت	*t*	As in *ten.*
ث	*th*	As in *thin.*
ج	*j*	As in *jewel.*
ح	*ḥ*	Tensely breathed *h* sound made by dropping tongue into back of throat, forcing the air out.
خ	*kh*	Pronounced like the *ch* in Scottish *loch*, made by touching back of tongue to roof of mouth and forcing air out.
د	*d*	As in *depth.*
ذ	*dh*	A thicker *th* sound as in *the.*
ر	*r*	A rolled *r*, similar to Spanish.
ز	*z*	As in *zest.*
س	*s*	As in *seen.*
ش	*sh*	As in *sheer.*
ص	*ṣ*	A heavy *s* pronounced far back in the mouth with the mouth hollowed to produce full sound.
ض	*ḍ*	A heavy *d/dh* pronounced far back in the mouth with the mouth hollowed to produce a full sound.
ط	*ṭ*	A heavy *t* pronounced far back in the mouth with the mouth hollowed to produce a full sound.
ظ	*ẓ*	A heavy *dh* pronounced far back in the mouth with the mouth hollowed to produce a full sound.
ع	ʿ	A guttural sound pronouned narrowing the throat.
غ	*gh*	Pronounced like a throaty French *r* with the mouth hallowed.
ف	*f*	As in *feel.*
ق	*q*	A guttural *q* sound made from the back of the throat with the mouth hallowed.
ك	*k*	As in *kit.*
ل	*l*	As in *lip.*
م	*m*	As in *melt.*
ن	*n*	As in *nest.*
ه	*h*	As in *hen.*

و	*w* (at the beg. of syllable)	As in *west.*
	ū (in the middle of syllable)	An elongated *oo* sound, as in *boo.*
ي	*y* (at beg. of syllable)	As in *yes.*
	ī (in the middle of syllable)	An elongated *ee* sound, as in *seen.*

- سبحانه وتعالى Used following the mention of Allah, God, translated as, "Glorified and Exalted be He."
- صلى الله عليه وسلم Used following the mention of the Prophet Muḥammad, translated as, "May God honor and protect him."
- عليه السلام Used following the mention of any other prophet or Gabriel, translated as, "May God's protection be upon him."
- رضي الله عنهم Used following the mention of the Prophet Muḥammad's Companions, translated as, "May God be pleased with them."
- رضي الله عنه Used following the mention of a male Companion of the Prophet Muḥammad, translated as, "May God be pleased with him."
- رضي الله عنها Used following the mention of a female Companion of the Prophet Muḥammad, translated as, "May God be pleased with her."
- رضي الله عنهما Used following the mention of two Companions of the Prophet Muḥammad, translated as, "May God be pleased with them both."
- رحمهم الله Used following the mention of the major scholars of Islam, translated as, "May God have mercy on them."
- رحمه الله Used following the mention of a major scholar of Islam, translated as, "May God have mercy on him."

INTRODUCTION
FROM THE AUTHOR

In the name of Allah the Most Merciful,
the Very Merciful.

Mu'āwiyah ؓ narrates that the Prophet ﷺ said:

مَنْ يُرِدِ اللَّهُ بِهِ خَيْرًا يُفَقِّهْهُ فِي الدِّينِ

*"Whomever Allah ﷻ intends good for He bestows upon them deep
understanding of religion."*[1]

If Allah ﷻ wants good for us in this world and the next, if He wants us to
be successful in this world leading a life according to His commands and
prohibitions, then He will give us a deep understanding of religion. Having
a deep, comprehensive, and insightful understanding of religion is an im-
mense blessing from Allah ﷻ. It is a sign that Allah ﷻ loves an individual
and wants them to succeed both in this life and in the life of the Hereafter.

The word dīn is usually used to refer to Islam in its entirety; its theology,

---

[1] Bukhārī, k. al-ʿilm, b. man yurid Allah bihī khayran yufaqqihu fī al-dīn, 71

morality, ethics, teachings, law, and ritual practices. That is why dīn is described as a complete way of life. This dīn is practiced through a divinely revealed system of law known as the Sharīʿah. Sharīʿah is what Allah ﷻ has legislated for His servants. It is God's revealed law that governs and regulates human life and activity. It is a complete system of life that we as believers have to follow in order to obtain guidance in this world and salvation in the next.

Oftentimes we understand Sharīʿah to be Islamic Law; however, that is only partially correct. The Sharīʿah is much more comprehensive than a legal code. It includes creed, ritual acts of worship, morals, ethics, and values. Although the common translation of "Islamic Law" is not completely wrong, it is under-inclusive; Islamic Law is only one aspect of the Sharīʿah.

Having said that, Islamic Law really has no parallel in history. It can be argued that it is the most successful and most widely practiced legal system in the world. For the last 1400 plus years it has been practiced by a number of different nations and communities that have strikingly different cultures and customs. One of the reasons for its success is first and foremost that it is divine. It is based on revelation from the Creator of the universe. Every other system of law is man-made and prone to faults, prejudices, deficiencies, injustices, and inequalities. The only system of law that can ensure equality, justice, and morality is the Sharīʿah. Who knows best how to govern human beings than the Creator Himself? It's the most comprehensive and complete way of life that deals with every type of relationship we as human beings can have. It deals with relationships between individuals, between individuals and the community, between different communities, between the individual and the Creator, and even between the community and the Creator. It's the law that governs the most beautiful way of life that's suitable for all times and places.

This system of law is based primarily on revelation, which includes both the Quran and Sunnah. The Quran and Sunnah provide a comprehensive code of law and teachings that are applicable and adaptable to all times, places, and circumstances. Throughout history, scholars developed a particular system and methodology built upon certain precepts and principles that are used to interpret the Quran and Sunnah. These principles and rules of interpretation provide a framework and methodology to derive laws from the primary sources. These precepts, principles, and rules are what make up the majority of Uṣūl al-Fiqh - Principles of Islamic Jurisprudence.

Uṣūl al-Fiqh is one of the most important yet most complex disciplines within Islamic Studies. Some scholars have written:

اِعلَمْ أَنَّ أُصولَ الفِقهِ مِنْ أَعظَمِ العُلُومِ الشَّرعِيَّةِ وَأَجَلِّهَا قَدرًا وأَكثَرِهَا فَائِدَةً

Realize that the knowledge of Uṣūl al-Fiqh is the greatest of Islamic Sciences, the highest in rank, and the most beneficial.

It's considered to be a unique contribution by Islam to the study of Law. There are two disciplines within Islamic Studies that are unique contributions of our scholars; Uṣūl al-Ḥadīth and Uṣūl al-Fiqh. In general, the study of Uṣūl al-Fiqh deals with the rules and principles jurists use to derive Islamic Law from its primary sources; the Quran, Sunnah, Ijmāʿ, and Qiyās. It's the discipline that tells us how law is derived from the Quran and Sunnah, how it's classified, understood, and applied. One of its main objectives is to provide jurists with a proper methodology for interpreting divine texts.

This short booklet will provide a brief history of the development and codification of Uṣūl al-Fiqh. It will examine the primary and secondary sources of Islamic Law, legal rulings, how they are derived and function, as well as a brief overview of the rules of interpretation. The main objective of this booklet is to introduce readers to the study of Uṣūl as well as create a deeper sense of appreciation for fiqh.

Alḥamdulillāh, through the grace and mercy of Allah ﷻ, I have been blessed with the opportunity to develop and teach a course through IOK Extension, which is now the part-time IOK Seminary, on Uṣūl al-Fiqh. While preparing for the course, I compiled a set of personal notes that I would use to teach the class. The course is also taught to the IOK Seminary students as an introduction and overview of the discipline. I thought that it would be beneficial for our students, as well as other students of knowledge, to compile my notes into a short booklet that can serve as a brief introduction to Uṣūl al-Fiqh in order to help establish a basic level of literacy within the subject. The purpose of this booklet is to provide, what I consider to be, something similar to "cliff notes" for Uṣūl al-Fiqh.

I compiled the notes primarily from seven sources:

1. *Principles of Islamic Jurisprudence* by Professor Hashim Kamali
2. *Outlines of Islamic Jurisprudence* by Dr. ʿImran Nyazee
3. *Islamic Jurisprudence: Usul al-Fiqh* by Dr. ʿImran Nyazee
4. *al-Wajīz fī Uṣūl al-Fiqh* by the late scholar Dr. Wahbah al-Zuḥaylī
5. *Uṣūl al-Fiqh al-Islāmī* also by Dr. Wahbah al-Zuḥaylī
6. *al-Mujaz fī Uṣūl al-Fiqh* by ʿUbayd Allāh Asadī
7. *Source Methodology in Islamic Jurisprudence* by Shaykh Taha Jabir al-ʿAlwani

This is not an original work; rather, it is a summary of what I found to be beneficial and important for beginning students of knowledge or for those interested in having a solid introduction to the study of Uṣūl al-Fiqh.

I would like to thank all of those individuals who provided suggestions, comments, improvements and took the time out of their busy schedules to edit this short work. May Allah ﷻ reward our IOK Seminary students Mudassir Mayet, Ayesha Hussain, and Munir Eltal, continue to bless them, and increase them in knowledge.

I ask Allah ﷻ to bless this small effort and make it beneficial for those who read it. I ask Allah ﷻ to bless all of us with a deep appreciation for the entire field of Fiqh and Uṣūl al-Fiqh and to increase our understanding of this beautiful religion. May Allah shower His blessings and mercy upon His last and final messenger, Muḥammad ﷺ.

Furhan Zubairi
Diamond Bar, CA
August 3, 2018 / Ṣafar 25, 1440

1

USUL AL-FIQH: TOOLS OF JURISPRUDENCE

Classical scholars would oftentimes start their works by mentioning some introductory points regarding the subject matter. This tradition is still carried on in Islamic seminaries and universities throughout the world where the instructor will give a brief overview of the subject matter before getting into greater detail. These preliminary remarks are termed al-mabādi', the fundamental concepts, which are the definition, subject matter, purpose, and objective of the discipline itself. These preliminary remarks provide a very general overview allowing the student to approach the discipline with a basic understanding of what is going to be studied.

DEFINITION

The scholars of Uṣūl al-Fiqh define the term using two different approaches. The first approach is to break the term down into its two individual parts, uṣūl and fiqh, and define each separately. The second is to define the term as a whole as the name given to a specific discipline or branch of knowledge within Islamic Studies.

Uṣūl al-Fiqh is a compound phrase made up of two words, uṣūl and fiqh. Uṣūl is the plural of aṣl, which is literally something upon which another thing is built or something from which another thing originates. It can mean root, origin, principle, proof, source, and foundation. The word is used here to convey the meaning of principles or proofs.

The word fiqh literally means to understand and to comprehend. Imām Abū Ḥanīfah ﷺ defined it as,

مَعرِفَةُ النَّفسِ مَا لَهَا وَمَا عَلَيهَا

An individual knowing their rights and responsibilities.

This is a very broad and general definition that is inclusive of articles of faith, laws of worship, and social interactions. As time progressed the definition of fiqh became more specific and refined. The more specific and refined technical definition of fiqh is,

العِلمُ بِالأَحكَامِ الشَّرعِيَّةِ العَمَلِيَّةِ المَكتَسَبَةِ مِن أَدِلَّتِهَا التَّفصِيلِيَّةِ

The knowledge of practical legal rulings derived from their detailed evidences.

It is the discipline of knowing and understanding Islamic Law. When defining terms, jurists are very specific and particular in their choice of words. They ensure that the definition is both exclusive (māniʿ), excluding everything extraneous, and inclusive (jāmiʿ), including everything necessary. "Knowledge of the practical legal rulings" refers to those laws associated to a person's actions or conduct. For example, it includes laws related to worship such as purification, prayer, and fasting as well as family and commercial law such as marriage, divorce, and contracts. It excludes knowledge related to the articles of faith, which is the subject matter of Creed (ʿAqīdah). The words "derived from their detailed evidences" refers to the fact that these laws are derived from specific texts of the Quran and Sunnah as well as other sources of law such as Ijmāʿ and Qiyās.

At this point it is also important to understand the definition of Sharīʿah because oftentimes the words fiqh and sharīʿah are used interchangeably. Linguistically, the word sharīʿah is derived from the root letters ش ر ع, which convey the meaning of coming to water to drink. Sharīʿah is defined as a watering hole or a drinking place: a place where a person or animal comes to drink water. Technically, it is defined as what Allah ﷻ has legislated for His servants from religion. Sharīʿah is God's revealed law that governs and regulates human life and activity. It is a code of life that believers follow in order to obtain guidance in this world and salvation in the next. Oftentimes, Sharīʿah is translated as Islamic Law; however, that is only partially correct. The Sharīʿah includes creed, ritual acts of worship, morals, ethics, and law. That is why a better understanding would be that the Sharīʿah is a complete code of life based on revealed scripture from God.

The most commonly accepted distinction between the two is that Sharīʿah is the revealed law found in the Quran and Sunnah and fiqh is a human understanding of that law. Sharīʿah is more general and inclusive; it includes both beliefs and deeds; whereas, fiqh deals with deeds alone.

As a branch of knowledge, jurists define Uṣūl al-Fiqh as the rules and principles a mujtahid[2] uses to derive practical legal rulings from their detailed evidences.[3] It is the set of rules, principles, and methodology of interpretation that have been defined in order to help a mujtahid derive legal rulings from textual evidences found in the Quran, Sunnah, and other sources of Islamic Law.[4] That is why it has been described as the methodology of law.

From this definition it can be understood that Fiqh is the end result of Uṣūl al-Fiqh. As mentioned earlier, Fiqh deals with the knowledge of the detailed rules of Islamic Law, and Uṣūl al-Fiqh deals with the way in which these rules are derived.

SUBJECT MATTER

Uṣūl al-Fiqh primarily deals with two things; the sources of Islamic Law and Islamic Law itself. The agreed upon sources of Islamic Law are the Quran, Sunnah, Ijmāʿ (Consensus), and Qiyās (Analogical Reasoning). In addition to these, there are a number of secondary sources that are not unanimously agreed upon. Jurists use evidences found in both the primary and secondary sources to derive legal rulings. Uṣūl al-Fiqh defines and describes these sources, how they indicate towards rulings, and how to interpret them. It lays

2 A mujtahid is a jurist who exercises ijtihād, the effort made in order to derive law, which is not self-evident, from its sources.

3 الْقَوَاعِدُ الَّتِي يَتَوَصَّلُ بِهَا الْمُجتَهِدُ إِلَى إِستَنبَاطِ الأَحكَامِ الشَّرعِيَّةِ العَمَلِيَّةِ مِن أَدِلَّتِهَا التَّفصِيلِيَّةِ

4 These will be discussed in later chapters.

down a structured methodology for juristic derivation and interpretation. It deals with the rules of interpretation.

With respect to Islamic Law, it deals with legal values such as obligation (wujūb), prohibition (ḥurmah), recommendation (nudb, istiḥbāb), permissibility (ibāḥah), and dislike (karāhah). It examines what they are, how they are defined, and how they are determined from the sources of law.

PURPOSE

The main purpose of Uṣūl al-Fiqh is to provide a mujtahid with the tools needed to derive legal rulings from textual sources. A mujtahid will be able to use these tools to understand and interpret texts from the Quran and Sunnah and show how they establish specific rulings.

As for a person who is not qualified to do ijtihād, then the study of Uṣūl al-Fiqh gives them the ability to understand how legal rules are derived from their sources. They will understand the methodology a mujtahid uses to arrive at their conclusions. They will be able to analyze and understand the reasoning behind rulings and how they were derived from their sources.

OBJECTIVE

The main objective behind studying any discipline within the field of Islamic Studies is to attain the pleasure of Allah ﷻ in order to be successful in this life and the next.

DERIVATION

Uṣūl al-Fiqh is, without a doubt, an independent field of study; however, it is based upon certain fundamental concepts that are derived from other fields of knowledge. Uṣūl al-Fiqh relies upon having a grounding in other academic disciplines which include, but are not limited to the following:

1. ʿIlm al-Kalām (Scholastic Theology): Who or what decides what is right or wrong? Is it the Sharīʿah itself or human reason? Can a person know what is right or wrong before revelation?
2. The Arabic Language: Words and how they are used to convey

meanings. Is the word explicit and clear or obscure and vague? Is the word specific or general, restricted or unrestricted? Is the word being used in its literal sense or is it being used metaphorically?

3. Manṭiq (Aristotelian Logic): The ways in which words convey their meanings as well as hermeneutics.
4. Classical Sciences of the Quran and Sunnah, such as discussions regarding the transmission of ḥadīth by a single narrator or by an impeccable plurality of narrators.

RULING

The study of Islamic Law and its principles or theory is considered to be a communal obligation. There must be some individuals in the community who are skilled in Islamic Law and its methodology.

2

HISTORY & DEVELOPMENT

The history and development of Uṣūl al-Fiqh and Fiqh in general passed through four primary eras:

1. The Era of the Prophet ﷺ
2. The Era of the Rightly Guided Caliphs ﷺ
3. The Era of the Companions ﷺ and elder Successors ﷺ
4. The Era of Codification

THE ERA OF THE PROPHET ﷺ

This era begins with Muḥammad ﷺ being appointed as the last and final messenger, thirteen years before the migration to Madinah, and ends with his leaving this world in the 11th year after migration. This era is considered to be the most important time in the development of Fiqh and Uṣūl al-Fiqh simply because it was the era of divine revelation.

Divine legislation, the law as revealed by Allah ﷻ and explained by His Messenger ﷺ, was completed during the lifetime of the Prophet ﷺ. As Allah ﷻ says in Sūrah al-Māʾidah, "Today I have perfected your religion for you, completed My favor upon you, and have approved Islam as your religion."[5]

---

5 5:3

The foundation of Fiqh throughout history has always been and will always be revelation, which is made up of both the Quran and Sunnah. This is a very important point to understand; revelation is not limited to the Quran. It also includes the Sunnah of the Prophet ﷺ. During the life of the Prophet ﷺ there were only two sources of law or legislation; the Quran and Sunnah.

The nature of revealed law in Makkah was very different than the nature of revealed law in Madinah. During the Makkan period, the first 13 years of the Prophet's ﷺ mission, revelation focused primarily on what is known as uṣūl al-dīn, the principles of religion. These are the fundamental aspects of belief; belief in the oneness of Allah ﷻ (tawḥīd), the concept of prophethood (risālah), and life after death (qiyāmah). It also includes morals, values, ethics, and character. For example, justice, fairness, excellence, gratitude, honesty, modesty, humility, patience, forbearance, and integrity. Makkan law focused on building the individual in terms of faith and character. During this time, only a few practical legal rulings were revealed and not in great detail. For example, ṣalāh and zakāh were legislated in Makkah but the specific rulings regarding them were not detailed.

The nature of revelation changed after migration. Madanī revelation focused heavily on detailed legal rulings of human actions. Verses were revealed regarding:

1. acts of worship such as ṣalāh, zakāh, fasting, and ḥajj
2. transactions such as sales, lease, other contracts, and the prohibition of interest
3. crimes such as murder theft, adultery, and false accusations
4. family law such as marriage, divorce, and inheritance
5. politics such as international relations and treaties

The Quran would lay down general principles for all these rulings and then the Prophet ﷺ would explain the particular details through his speech, actions, and approvals.

However, the Prophet ﷺ would not explain every minute detail as is done today in the books of Fiqh. He ﷺ would not say that the farā'iḍ (necessary parts) of wuḍū' (ritual purification) are four, and these are the sunnan (prophetic recommendations), and these are the mustaḥabbāt (extra recommendations). Rather, the Companions رضي الله عنهم would see the Messenger ﷺ

perform wuḍū' and do it exactly as he did. They would watch him perform ṣalah (ritual prayer) and then pray just like him. They performed ḥajj with him and learned the rites of ḥajj through observation.

Another unique feature of this era is that the law was not revealed all at once. It was revealed gradually over a period of 23 years, slowly taking shape. For example, initially prayer was an obligation in the morning and the evening and later on it was made obligatory five times a day. Initially the amount of zakāh was not set; it was up to the individual to pay how much they were able to or wanted to. Similarly, intoxicating drinks were not outright forbidden; rather, the prohibition went through a gradual process. Some laws were revealed in response to certain events that took place or questions posed to the Prophet ﷺ. Others were revealed without a specific cause or question. It is crucial to realize that the source of all these laws was revelation; either directly through the Quran or indirectly through the Sunnah of the Prophet ﷺ.

During this time the Prophet ﷺ also exercised his own ijtihād as did some of his Companions رضي الله عنهم. Mu'ādh ibn Jabal رضي الله عنه narrated that when the Prophet ﷺ sent him to Yemen he asked, "How will you judge when a new situation comes up?" He replied, "I will judge in accordance with Allah's Book." He asked, "What will you do if you don't find anything stated in Allah's Book?" He replied, "I'll act in accordance with the Sunnah of the Messenger of Allah ﷺ." He asked, "What if you do not find anything stated in the Sunnah of the Messenger of Allah ﷺ and in Allah's Book?" He replied, "I'll do my best to form an opinion (based on them) and I'll exhaust my full effort." The Messenger of Allah ﷺ then patted him on the chest and said, "Praise be to Allah Who has helped the messenger of the Messenger of Allah to find something which pleases the Messenger of Allah."[6]

Ijtihād in this period was still considered to be a part of revelation. Whenever the Prophet ﷺ exercised his own judgment Allah ﷻ would either affirm it or guide him to something better. If there was a better judgment, Allah ﷻ would reveal that the better solution was other than that which he had chosen. At times, Allah ﷻ would make the better judgement binding, and at times Allah ﷻ would let the ruling of the Prophet ﷺ stand.

As for the Companions رضي الله عنهم, they would perform ijtihād in response to situations that they faced in the absence of the Prophet ﷺ. Later, when they

---

6 Abū Dāwūd, *k. al-aqḍiyah, b. ijtihād al-ra'y fī al-qaḍā'a*, 3592

met the Prophet ﷺ they would explain what happened and tell him what they had decided. Sometimes the Prophet ﷺ would approve their conclusions, in which case they would become part of the Sunnah. If he did not approve of their conclusions, he would explain what was better and that would become a part of the Sunnah.

In summary, during this time, legislation depended on two forms of divine revelation:

1. Recited Revelation (Quran)
2. Non-recited Revelation (Sunnah)

In terms of codification, the Quran was recorded in its entirety during the life of the Prophet ﷺ; however, it was not compiled into a single book. Some of the Companions ﵃ used to write down aḥadīth of the Prophet ﷺ, but it would be their own personal notes or collections.

THE ERA OF THE RIGHTLY GUIDED CALIPHS

This era started after the Prophet ﷺ left this world in the year 11 A.H. and lasted for around 30 years, until 40 A.H. As mentioned earlier, divine revelation was complete during the time of the Prophet ﷺ in the form of the Quran and Sunnah and they served as the primary sources for the legal judgments and rulings of the jurists among the Companions. During this era the primary sources of Islamic Law were:

1. The Quran
2. The Sunnah
3. Ijmāʿ (Consensus)
4. Ijtihād (Personal Opinion)

Two new sources of Islamic Law, Ijmāʿ and Qiyās, naturally evolved and developed. As Muslim society progressed and expanded, the Companions faced situations and problems that they did not face during the time of the Prophet ﷺ and it was necessary for them to determine the legal rulings for them. The jurists (fuqahāʾ) amongst the companions took on the responsibility of determining the rulings of these new issues and occurrences, using their skills of reasoning in the light of the Quran and Sunnah.

Their methodology was straightforward and built upon the methodology that the Prophet ﷺ approved for Muʿādh ؓ when he sent him to Yemen. If something new came up they would first look to the Quran. If they could not find the ruling in the Quran they would turn to the Sunnah of the Prophet ﷺ. If they could not find the ruling in the aḥadīth then they would gather the companions and try to reach a collective decision. If no collective decision was reached, the jurist companion would formulate and develop their own opinion.

This methodology was captured by Maymūn ibn Mahrān when he summarized Abū Bakr's ؓ methodology of arriving at legal judgments. "Whenever a dispute was referred to him, Abū Bakr ؓ used to look in the Quran; if he found something according to which he could pass a judgment, he did so. If he could not find a solution in the Quran, but remembered some relevant aspect of the Prophet's Sunnah, he would judge according to that. If he could find nothing in the Sunnah, he would go and say to the Muslims: 'Such and such a dispute has been referred to me. Do any of you know anything in the Prophet's Sunnah according to which judgment may be passed?' If someone was able to answer his question and provide relevant information, Abū Bakr ؓ would say: 'Praise be to Allah Who has enabled some of us to remember what they have learnt from our Prophet.' If he could not find any solution in the Sunnah, then he would gather the leaders and elite of the Companions and consult with them. If they agreed on the matter then he passed judgment on that basis. If none of the above resulted in a satisfactory answer he would then do ijtihād and form his own opinion. When Abu Bakr ؓ would form his own opinion he would say, 'This is my opinion. If it is correct then it is from Allah and if it is wrong then it is from me and I seek forgiveness from Allah.'"[7] From this quote it can be seen that his methodology was Quran, Sunnah, Ijmāʿ, and exercising personal opinion (raʾy) based on legal reasoning (qiyās) or benefit (maṣlaḥah).

ʿUmar ibn al-Khaṭṭāb ؓ followed pretty much the exact same methodology in arriving at rulings and judgments. He wrote to one of his judges, Shurayḥ, "If you find something in the book of Allah then judge according to it and do not turn towards anything else. If something comes to you that is not in the book of Allah then judge according to what the Messenger

---

7 al-Jawzī, *ʿAlām al-Muwaqqʿīn*, 1:65

of Allah 🌸 established as a Sunnah. If something comes to you that is not in the book of Allah or the Sunnah of the Messenger of Allah 🌸 then judge according to what the people have agreed upon. If something comes to you that is not in the book of Allah, nor in the Sunnah of the Messenger of Allah 🌸 nor has anyone spoken about it before you, then if you must exercise your own judgment, do so, and if you can refrain, then refrain. And refraining is better for you."[8] Something very similar is also narrated from ibn Masʿūd 🌸 and ibn ʿAbbās 🌸.

These narrations clearly show that the jurists amongst the Companions of the Prophet 🌸 pretty much followed the same methodology in deriving rulings for new issues that they faced.

Now, it is important to understand what exactly is meant by raʾy: personal opinion. Raʾy is inclusive of many things that were given very specific technical names later on such as analogical reasoning (qiyās), public benefit (maṣlaḥah), and precautionary prohibitions (sad al-dharāʾiʿ). The Companions of the Prophet 🌸 had a very clear methodology that they adopted in order to issue legal verdicts (fatāwā). Sometimes they were based on public interest or taking precautions to prevent wrongdoing.

Not all the Companions of the Prophet 🌸 were considered to be jurists or qualified to give legal rulings. There are about 130 Companions, both male and female, who were known to have given fatwā. There were seven who gave more fatāwā than others:

1. ʿUmar ibn al-Khaṭṭāb
2. ʿAlī ibn Abī Ṭālib
3. ʿAbdullāh ibn Masʿūd
4. ʿĀʾishah
5. Zayd ibn Thābit
6. ʿAbdullāh ibn ʿAbbās
7. ʿAbdullāh ibn ʿUmar 🌸

Then there were others who gave less, such as Abū Bakr, ʿUthmān ibn ʿAffān, and Abū Mūsā al-Ashʿarī 🌸.

Amongst the Companions 🌸 there were two attitudes towards using raʾy; those who employed it frequently and those who employed it sparingly.

---

8   al-Jawzī, ʿAlām al-Muwaqqʿīn, 1:66

It can be said that this was the initial foundation of the two main schools of thought or legal methodology that emerged in the third era, the School of Ḥadīth and the School of Ra'y. This attitude was not necessarily related to how they viewed ra'y, it was more of a personal choice.

This difference in approach was even seen during the time of the Prophet ﷺ as is highlighted in the famous ḥadīth of Banū Qurayẓah. The Prophet ﷺ told his Companions, "Do not pray ʿaṣr prayer until you reach Banū Qurayẓah [a Jewish fortress on the outskirts of Madīnah]." A group of them were delayed on the way and the time for ʿaṣr prayer was almost finished. Some of them decided not to pray until they arrived, taking the Prophet's words literally. Others from the group insisted: "We will pray. The Prophet ﷺ didn't mean that we should skip the prayer." After they arrived, they informed the Prophet what had happened, and he didn't criticize either of them for what they did.[9]

Whenever there is ijtihād, it is natural for there to be disagreements. Another jurist will either agree with the conclusion or disagree with it. It should not be surprising that there were differences of opinion amongst the Companions ﷺ, but their differences were few and rare.

During this time period the Quran was compiled into a single book and copies of it were sent across the Muslim world, which had expanded well beyond the Arabian Peninsula. The aḥadīth of the Prophet ﷺ were still not formally codified and compiled at this time.

THE ERA OF THE COMPANIONS AND THE ELDER SUCCESSORS

This era began after the time of the Rightly Guided Caliphs, around the year 41 A.H and lasted until the beginning of the second century A.H., right before the fall of the Umayyad Dynasty. Legislation during this time period was very similar to what it was during the time of the Companions ﷺ; the methodology of the Companions ﷺ and their students, the Tābiʿūn ﷺ, in deriving legal rulings was very similar. They would first look to the Quran, then the Sunnah, then Ijmāʿ and lastly Qiyās.

During this time period Muslim society progressed and expanded even more, bringing about many unprecedented issues and cases that needed to

9 Bukhārī, *k. ṣalāh al-khawf, b. ṣalāh al-ṭālib wa al-maṭlūb rākiban wa īmā'an*, 946

have legal rulings and Islamic guidance. With the growth and expansion of Islamic lands, there was a need for individuals to go to these new places to teach people their new religion.

During and after the time of ʿUthmān ﵁ many of the jurists amongst the Companions of the Prophet ﷺ were sent to different parts of the Islamic world as teachers and judges. There were six major centers of the Islamic world and each center had recognized teachers and authorities who were either companions or their students:

1. **Makkah:** ʿAbdullāh ibn ʿAbbās ﵄
2. **Madinah:** ʿAbdullāh ibn ʿUmar ﵄, Mujāhid ibn Jabr ﵀, ʿAṭāʾ ibn Abī Rabāḥ ﵀, and Ṭāwūs ibn Kaysān ﵀
3. **Kūfah:** ʿAbdullāh ibn Masʿūd ﵁, ʿAlqamah al-Nakhaʿī ﵀, al-Aswad ibn Yazīd ﵀, and Ibrāhīm al-Nakhaʿī ﵀
4. **Baṣrah:** Abū Mūsā al-Ashʿarī ﵁, Anas ibn Mālik ﵁, Muḥammad ibn Sīrīn ﵀
5. **Shām (Levant):** Muʿādh ibn Jabal ﵁, ʿUbādah ibn al-Ṣāmit ﵁, Abū Idrīs al-Khawlānī ﵀, and ʿUmar ibn ʿAbd al-ʿAzīz ﵀
6. **Miṣr (Egypt):** ʿAbdullāh ibn ʿAmr ibn al-ʿĀṣ ﵄

The development of fiqh and legislation and its expansion during this era can be attributed to three main factors:

1. WIDENING OF THE SCOPE AND APPLICATION OF FIQH AND INCREASE IN DIFFERENCES

The scope of fiqh expands and grows with the occurrence of new events, incidents, and circumstances and these constantly change depending on the time and place. In addition to that, Islam had spread to foreign lands that had their own unique customs, traditions, societal, and economic practices. Every jurist took into consideration the circumstances and society they lived in when giving rulings as long as it didn't go against the Sharīʿah.

2. SPREADING OF THE NARRATION OF ḤADĪTH

During the time of the Prophet ﷺ and the Rightly Guided Caliphs the narration of aḥadīth was limited as compared to later times. As the Companions ﵃ spread across the Muslim world so too did the narration of aḥadīth. Not every Companion was equal when it came to aḥadīth, some had memorized more than others. Some had heard more than others and some narrated more than others. The increase in narration of ḥadīth had a large impact on Fiqh and the derivation of legal rulings. Narrations were being used more often to derive and establish rulings.

3. THE EMERGENCE OF THE TRADITIONALISTS (AHL AL-ḤADĪTH) AND THE RATIONALISTS (AHL AL-RA'Y)

As mentioned earlier, the jurists amongst the Companions ﷽ can be divided into two broad categories; those who were extremely hesitant in doing their own ijtihād and expressing their own personal opinion using it sparingly, and those who would do their own ijtihād whenever the need would arise. The first group feared contradicting the letter of the Quran and Sunnah so they were hesitant in going beyond what the text said.

During this time period both of these tendencies became more defined and their methodologies started to become more refined. This led to the emergence of two informal schools of legal thought or methodology, the Rationalists (Ahl al-Ra'y) and the Traditionalists (Ahl al-Ḥadīth). There were differences between them concerning source methodology and issues of case law. Both of these schools had their origins in the approaches of the Companions ﷽, but it was during this time that their differences in matters of fiqh became clear. Slowly, people started grouping themselves on the basis of their differences in deriving legal rulings from their sources.

Historians write that the Traditionalist School was a continuation of those Companions whose fear of contradicting the letter of the Quran and Sunnah made them hesitant with respect to exercising their own personal opinion. For example, ʿAbdullāh ibn ʿUmar ﷽ and ʿAbdullāh ibn ʿAbbās ﷽. The Traditionalist School became widespread in the Ḥijāz and specifically Madīnah. It can be said that the Traditionalist School organically developed and evolved into the School of Madīnah, which then developed into the School of Imām Mālik ﷽. One of the reasons why it became widespread in Madīnah is because of the abundance of aḥadīth and familiarity with the fatāwā of a number of Companions.

The leading scholar of this camp was al-Imām Saʿīd ibn al-Musayyab ﷽ (d. 94). There were seven successors who are considered to be the seven jurists of Madinah who carried on the teachings of the Companions from that area:

1. ʿUrwah ibn Zubair (d. 94)
2. Saʿīd ibn al-Musayyab (d. 94)
3. al-Qasim ibn Muḥammad (d. 94)
4. Abū Bakr ibn ʿAbd al-Raḥmān ibn al-Ḥārith (d. 94)
5. ʿUbaydullāh ibn ʿAbdillah ibn ʿUtbah ibn Masʿūd (d. 98)
6. Khārijah ibn Zayd (d. 99)
7. Sulaymān ibn Yasār (d. 107)

They were known as the Seven Jurists (al-Fuqahāʾ al-Sabʿah). As mentioned above their methodology and approach continued to evolve and develop culminating in the School of Imām Mālik ﷺ.

The Rationalist School was an extension of the school of ʿUmar ibn al-Khaṭṭāb and ʿAbdullāh ibn Masʿūd ﷺ, who were the most exercising of ijtihād. ʿAlqamah ibn Qays al-Nakhaʿī (d. 62) was influenced by them, the uncle and teacher of Ibrāhīm al-Nakhaʿī, who taught Ḥammād ibn Abī Sulaymān, who was the teacher of Imām Abū Ḥanīfah ﷺ. The Rationalist School gained popularity in Iraq and organically developed into what is known as the School of Kūfah. The School of Kūfah was the foundation for the School of Imām Abū Ḥanīfah ﷺ.

The jurists in this camp felt that legal interpretations should not be limited to the letter of the texts but also the spirit. They felt it was their responsibility to uncover the intended meanings and wisdoms behind the laws and to make connections between them. The reason why this methodology became popular in Iraq is because of the number of Companions who were influenced by ʿUmar ibn al-Khaṭṭāb ﷺ.

Both of these informal schools agreed on the importance and status of aḥadīth within the framework of Islamic Law and accepted that it was the most important source of law after the Quran. At the same time, the Traditionalists also agreed with the Rationalists on the need for having recourse to reason and ijtihād for those issues that were not explicitly mentioned in the Quran and ḥadīth.

THE ERA OF THE MUJTAHID IMAMS AND CODIFICATION

This era started in the beginning of the second century A.H. and lasted till about the middle of the fourth century A.H. During this time period Fiqh as a discipline went through expansive growth and refinement. It flourished and developed into an independent discipline. This was the era of expert jurists, the great mujtahids, who laid down the foundations of their respective schools of thought. Every school of thought in reality is a juristic methodology of approaching the Quran and Sunnah and extracting rules from them. This was also the era of the great scholars of ḥadīth. Both the study of fiqh and ḥadīth were codified and became disciplines that were taught and studied. Books were compiled and written. Because of all this advancement in the field of Islamic Studies, this era is known as the Golden Era of Fiqh, the Era of Codification, and the Era of the Mujtahidūn.

This expansive growth and development can be attributed to a number of different factors:

1. THE ʿABBĀSID CALIPHS GAVE A LOT OF CARE AND IMPORTANCE TO FIQH AND FUQAHĀʾ

The ʿAbbāsid Caliphs were fond of jurists and would consult them fairly often. For example, the Caliph Manṣūr tried to convince Imām Mālik ﷺ to make his *Muwaṭṭaʾ* the official book of law for the Caliphate. The Caliph Hārūn al-Rashīd had asked Imām Abū Yūsuf ﷺ, the famous student of Imām Abū Ḥanīfah ﷺ, to establish a system of laws for the financial affairs of the state. In response he wrote his famous book al-Kharaj. This care and importance from the government level allowed the jurists to flourish.

2. THE EXPANSIVENESS OF THE MUSLIM STATE

Muslim rule stretched all the way from Spain to China. This added a lot of richness and diversity to fiqh. Each area faced its own unique circumstances, issues, conditions, and culture that played a role in the development and advancement of Fiqh.

3. THE WORK OF THE GREAT MUJTAHID IMĀMS

Imām Abū Ḥanīfah, Imām Mālik, Imām al-Shāfiʿī, and Imām Aḥmad ﷺ.

4. THE CODIFICATION OF ḤADĪTH

By this time a number of the most famous collections of ḥadīth had been compiled and authored. One of the earliest works is the *Muwaṭṭaʾ* of Imām Mālik ﵀. This era marked a new phase in the development and documentation of ḥadīth. One of the most distinctive features of this period was to separate the aḥadīth of the Prophet ﷺ from the sayings of the Companions and Successors. The ḥadīth compilers of this era largely observed the principles of Uṣūl al-Ḥadīth that had already gained recognition and the methodological guidelines that were developed. This was the era in which ḥadīth studies flourished and books on different disciplines were written.

It was in the second half of this century that the six most famous and well-recognized books of ḥadīth were compiled: *Ṣaḥīḥ al-Bukhārī*, *Ṣaḥīḥ Muslim*, *Jāmiʿ al-Tirmidhī*, *Sunan Abī Dāwūd*, *Sunan ibn Mājah*, and *Sunan al-Nasāʾī*. These books make up the six canonical books of ḥadīth known as al-Ṣiḥāḥ al-Sittah (The Six Authentic Books) or al-Kutub al-Sittah (The Six Books).

Through the tireless effort of the luminaries of the first three centuries of Islam, the Sunnah of the Prophet ﷺ was gathered, analyzed, organized, codified, and preserved for future generations. Many of these works have been passed on from generation to generation and are still read, studied, explained, and commented on in seminaries and universities throughout the world.

5. THE EMERGENCE OF THE FORMAL LEGAL SCHOOLS OF THOUGHT

As mentioned earlier, the School of Abū Ḥānīfah ﵀ emerged from the School of Kūfah, and the School of Imām Mālik ﵀ was born out of the School of Madīnah. Imām al-Shāfiʿī ﵀ was influenced heavily by both schools, being a student of both Imām Mālik ﵀ and Imām Muḥammad ibn Ḥasan al-Shaybānī ﵀, one of the foremost students of Abū Ḥanīfah ﵀. He then developed his own methodology and framework for deriving Fiqh from its sources. The first person to write a book on Uṣūl al-Fiqh is Imām al-Shāfiʿī ﵀. That is why he is considered to be the father of Uṣūl al-Fiqh. The School of Imām Aḥmad ﵀ was born from the School of Ḥadīth, the Traditionalists.

Each school of thought produced its own jurists who would then produce works that served as the basis of future works within the same school. Each school specified its methodology for interpreting texts and deriving legal rulings from them. Each school developed an independent set of principles and methodology that it used to derive legal rulings from the Quran, Sunnah, Ijmāʿ, and Qiyās. Due to many factors (beyond the scope of this text), only four schools of thought gained widespread acceptance and prominence:

1. Ḥanafī
2. Mālikī
3. Shāfiʿī
4. Ḥanbalī

It is through the tireless efforts of these amazing jurists that Fiqh was codified, organized, and preserved for future generations. Many of their works have been passed on from generation to generation and are still read, studied, explained, and commented on to this day.

PART 1:

THE LEGAL RULING

3

AL-HUKM AL-SHAR'I: THE LEGAL RULING

Al-Aḥkām al-Sharʿiyyah is the plural of al-Ḥukm al-Sharʿī, which is translated as "the legal ruling". A legal ruling can broadly be understood as a command, prohibition, recommendation, or discouragement from Allah ﷻ that informs, governs, and regulates human behavior. It addresses questions such as "what is permissible?", "what is impermissible?", "what is recommended?", and, "what is disliked?". They are the rules that make up Islamic law. The purpose of studying the "legal ruling" is to understand the conceptual part of Islamic Law. It helps clarify, explain, conceptualize, and explore the question, "what is Islamic Law?" These are legal values that are used to categorize and classify human conduct and behavior.

ELEMENTS OF A HUKM SHAR'I

When discussing the "legal value" or the legal ruling it is important to understand that there are four aspects to it. These four parts can be considered as the players involved in the ḥukm.

1. al-Ḥākim (الحَاكِمُ): The Lawgiver or the ultimate source from which law originates. The ultimate source of Islamic Law is Allah ﷻ, and by extension the Prophet ﷺ.

2. al-Maḥkūm fīh (المَحكُومُ فِيهِ): The act or object upon which the ruling applies.
3. al-Maḥkūm ʿalayh (المَحكُومُ عَلَيهِ): The person for whom the law is given.
4. al-Ḥukm (الحُكمُ): The actual law or ruling itself.

AL-HUKM (الحُكمُ): **THE COMMAND**

The word ḥukm literally means rule or command. According to the scholars of Uṣūl al-Fiqh, a ḥukm (legal rule) is defined as:

خِطَابُ اللّٰهِ تَعَالَى المُتَعَلِّقُ بِأَفعَالِ المُكَلَّفِينَ بِالاِقتِضَاءِ أَو التَّخيِيرِ أَو الوَضعِ

God's address in relation to the acts of the legally responsible[10] *through a command, option, or declaration.*

The first part of the definition "a communication or address from Allah (خطاب الله)" refers to the speech of Allah ﷻ directly through the Quran or indirectly through the Sunnah of the Prophet ﷺ. It is a verse of the Quran or a ḥadīth of the Prophet ﷺ of a legal nature.

The second part of the definition "related to the acts of the legally responsible (المتعلق بأفعال المكلفين)" refers to that fact that this communication or address has to be related to an action that human beings can do such as prayer, fasting, charity, theft, lawful and unlawful intercourse (zinā), etc. It is a directive from Allah ﷻ concerned with the conduct of human beings. This ḥukm, which is a communication from Allah ﷻ in the form of a verse from the Quran or ḥadīth of the Prophet ﷺ, can be expressed through a command, choice, or declaration.

The third part of the definition "through a command (بالاقتضاء)" means that the ḥukm is expressed through a command or prohibition. This can be a command to either do something or a prohibition to shun something. This command can be expressed in definitive binding terms, meaning the act has

10 Legally responsible, or mukallaf, refers to an individual who is adult and sane.

to be done, creating an obligation. The command can also be expressed in terms that are not absolute or binding. In such a scenario the ḥukm serves as a recommendation. The jurists use various rules to determine when a command is expressed in binding or non-binding terms. Similarly, the prohibition can be in clear and explicit terms resulting in impermissibility or it can be in non-binding terms resulting in dislike.

The fourth part of the definition "option (التخيير)" means that the ḥukm is expressed as a choice; the individual has the option to do it or leave it, both being permissible. Meaning, a person is free to choose if they want to do the action or not, it is completely up to their discretion. This gives rise to the concept of permissibility.

The fifth part of the definition "declaration (الوضع)" means that the ḥukm is expressed as a declaration. The Law Maker declares one thing to be the cause of another (sabab), or a condition for it (sharṭ), or an impediment (māniʿ), or declares the action to be valid or invalid.

In summary, a ḥukm, a legal ruling (rule of law), is the speech of Allah ﷻ addressed to human beings as a command, choice, or declaration. This legal rule can be a verse from the Quran, a ḥadīth of the Prophet ﷺ, consensus (Ijmāʿ), or even analogical reasoning (Qiyās).

Example 1:

يَا أَيُّهَا الَّذِينَ آمَنُوا أَوْفُوا بِالْعُقُودِ

"O you who have believed, fulfill [all] contracts."[11]

This statement of Allah ﷻ is a legal ruling because it is a communication of Allah concerning the conduct of an individual who is legally responsible. The verse explicitly and clearly commands believers to fulfill their contracts.

Example 2:

وَأَقِيمُوا الصَّلَاةَ وَآتُوا الزَّكَاةَ وَارْكَعُوا مَعَ الرَّاكِعِينَ

[Allah ﷻ says,] "And establish ṣalāḥ (prayer) and give zakāh (charity) and make rukū' (bow) with those who bow [in worship and obedience]."[12]

11 5:1

12 2:43

This verse is also a legal ruling because it is an address from Allah ﷻ concerning the conduct of a legally responsible individual. It commands believers to establish prayer and pay zakāh.

Example 3:

وَلَا تَقْرَبُوا الزِّنَا ۖ إِنَّهُ كَانَ فَاحِشَةً وَسَاءَ سَبِيلًا

[Allah ﷻ says,] "And do not even approach unlawful sexual intercourse (zinā). It is completely immoral, and wicked in nature."[13]

This verse is considered to be a legal ruling. It is an address from the Lawgiver concerning the action of an individual who is legally responsible. It prohibits the believers from coming close to unlawful intercourse.

Example 4:

الْقَاتِلُ لاَ يَرِث

[The Prophet ﷺ said,] "The killer does not inherit."[14]

This is an example of a ḥadīth that is a legal ruling.

Example 5:

لاَ يَقْبَلُ اللَّهُ صَلاَةَ أَحَدِكُمْ إِذَا أَحْدَثَ حَتَّى يَتَوَضَّأَ

[The Prophet ﷺ said,] "Allah ﷻ doesn't accept your prayer, if you've broken your wuḍūʾ, until you purify yourselves."[15]

From this ḥadīth jurists derive the rule that purification is a precondition for the validity of prayer.

From this technical definition, the scholars of Uṣūl divide a ḥukm (legal rule) into two categories:

---

13 17:32

14 Tirmidhī, *k. al-farāʾid*, 2255, - Abū Dāwūd, *k. al-diyāt b. diyāt al-aʿḍāʾ*, 4564, - Ibn Mājah, *k. al-diyāt*, 2747 and *k. al-farāʾid*, 2840

15 Bukhārī, *k. al-ḥiyal b. fī al-ṣalāh*, 6954

1. al-Ḥukm al-Taklīfiy (Defining Law) and
2. al-Ḥukm al-Waḍʿiy (Declaratory Law). That is because the communication from Allah ﷻ is expressed as a command, choice, or declaration. If it is expressed as a command or choice then it is considered to be a ḥukm taklīfiy and if it is a declaration it is considered to be a ḥukm waḍʿiy.

AL-HUKM AL-TAKLIFIY (الحُكمُ التَّكلِيفِيُّ): DEFINING LAW

Al-Ḥukm al-Taklīfiy is usually translated as defining law because it defines the extent or limit of an individual's liberty of action. It defines what a person can and can't do; what a person has to do, what they should do, what they shouldn't do, and what they have a choice to do. It is a ḥukm that requires the mukallaf to either do something, avoid doing something, or the choice to either do it or not. In technical terms, it is a communication from Allah ﷻ that commands the mukallaf to do something or forbids them from doing something, or gives them the option between the two.

For example, Allah ﷻ says, "And establish the prayer".[16] This is a legal ruling that commands an individual that is legally responsible to do something, which is pray. Similarly, Allah ﷻ says, "Fasting has been made obligatory upon you."[17] This is a legal ruling that commands a mukallaf to fast. An example of a legal ruling that forbids doing something is, "And do not even approach unlawful sexual intercourse."[18] This is a legal ruling the prohibits a person from engaging in unlawful sexual intercourse.

This type of ḥukm is divided into the five well-known categories:

1. Farḍ / Wājib (Obligatory)
2. Sunnah / Mustaḥab / Mandūb (Recommended)
3. Ḥarām (Forbidden)
4. Makrūh (Disliked)
5. Mubāḥ / Ḥalāl (Permissible)

---

16 2:43
17 2:183
18 17:32

The Ḥanafī's divide it into seven categories:

1. Farḍ (obligatory)
2. Wājib (Mandatory)
3. Mandūb (Recommended)
4. Makrūh Tanzīhan (Slightly Disliked)
5. Makrūh Taḥrīman (Prohibitively Disliked)
6. Ḥarām (Prohibited)
7. Mubāḥ (Permissible)

AL-HUKM AL-WAD'IY (الحُكم الوَضعِيّ): **DECLARATORY LAW**

Al-Ḥukm al-Waḍʿiy is usually translated as Declaratory Law. It is defined as a communication from Allah that enacts something into a cause, condition, or a hindrance to something else. It is a ḥukm that declares the legal relationship between the cause (sabab) and its effect (musabbab) or between the precondition (sharṭ) and its object (mashrūṭ).

For example, Allah ﷻ says, "So whoever sights [the new moon of] the month, let him fast it."[19] In this verse Allah ﷻ clarifies that sighting the moon is the cause (sabab) for fasting becoming an obligation (musabbab). Similarly, the Prophet ﷺ said, "Allah ﷻ doesn't accept a prayer without purification." From this ḥadīth, jurists derive that purification is a precondition (sharṭ) for the validity of prayer.

Al-Ḥukm al-Waḍʿiy is usually divided into five categories as well:

1. Sabab (Cause)
2. Sharṭ (Precondition)
3. Māniʿ (Hindrance)
4. ʿAzīmah (strict Law) as opposed to Rukhṣah (Concession)
5. Ṣaḥiḥ (Valid) as opposed to Bāṭil (Null)

AL-WAJIB (الوَاجِب): **OBLIGATORY**

Something that is wājib is technically defined as,

19 2:185

هُوَ مَا طَلَبَ الشَّارِعُ فِعلَهُ مِن المُكَلَّفِ طَلَبًا حَتمًا

An act the Lawgiver commands a mukallaf to do in certain and binding terms.

The certain and binding nature of the command is either understood from the syntax, context, or language of the statement as well as from external evidence. Examples of acts that are wājib are praying, fasting, paying zakāh, ḥajj, and fulfilling contracts.

When something is wājib it has to be done. The one who does it will be rewarded and the one who chooses not to is liable and deserving of punishment. According to the majority of jurists there is no difference between the terms farḍ and wājib; they are synonymous.

The Ḥanafī's differentiate between the two. According to them, something that is farḍ is defined as an act that is established by a definitive proof (دَلِيلٌ قَطعِيٌّ) whose meaning is definite and not open to the possibility of interpretation, and is undeniably authentic. A definitive proof is textual evidence that is definitive both in terms of its authenticity and meaning. For example, a verse of the Quran, a mutawātir (mass unchallenged) ḥadīth, or a mashūr (widely transmitted) ḥadīth. When something is farḍ, an individual must believe that it is obligatory and is also required to act upon it. If a person does something that is farḍ they will be rewarded, and if they choose not to then they will be liable and deserving of punishment. A person who denies that something is farḍ can be taken out of the fold of Islam. Therefore, there is both a theological as well as a practical aspect to something that is farḍ. Examples of acts that are considered to be farḍ are the five daily prayers, fasting, ḥajj, and zakāh.

According to the Ḥanafī's something that is considered to be wājib is defined as an act established by a speculative proof (دَلِيلٌ ظَنِّيٌّ) that has room for interpretation. A speculative proof is textual evidence that is speculative either in its authenticity, its meaning, or in both. For example, solitary narrations (khabar al-wāḥid) are speculative in terms of authenticity, but they can either be definitive or speculative in terms of meaning. Just like an act that is farḍ, there is a theological as well as a practical aspect. When something is wājib an individual is required to act upon it, but they don't necessarily have to believe that it is mandatory. If a person does it they will be rewarded, and if they choose not to, then they will be liable and deserving of punishment. Practically speaking, there is no difference between something that is farḍ and something that is wājib. The difference is in how the act is established through textual evidence and its theological implications. Examples of acts that are considered to be wājib are ṣadaqah al-fiṭr, ʿĪd prayer, and the Witr prayer.

AL-MANDUB (المَندُوبُ): **RECOMMENDED**

Linguistically, the word mandūb is defined as a call towards an act or a recommendation. According to the scholars of Uṣūl, it is defined as a command from the Lawgiver to do an act without making it binding and without assigning blame for not doing it.

هُوَ مَا طَلَبَ الشَّارِعُ فِعلَهُ مِن المُكَلَّفِ طَلَبًا غيرَ حَتمٍ

It is an act the Lawgiver commands a mukallaf to do in non-binding terms.

The non-binding nature of the command is understood from the syntax, grammar, or context as well as from external evidence. For example, the Prophet ﷺ said, "Whoever makes wuḍū' on Friday then it suffices and it's good, and whoever bathes, then bathing is better."[20] From this ḥadīth, jurists conclude that it is recommended (sunnah) for one to take a ritual bath for Friday prayer.

Recommended Acts are then classified into two broad categories:

1. AL-SUNNAH AL-MU'AKKADAH (السُّنَّةُ المُؤَكَّدَةُ): RELIGIOUSLY EMPHASIZED SUNNAH

al-Sunnah al-Mu'akkadah is a recommended act that was done by the Prophet ﷺ on a regular and consistent basis while leaving it occasionally,

20 مَنْ تَوَضَّأَ يَوْمَ الْجُمُعَةِ فَبِهَا وَنِعْمَتْ وَمَنِ اغْتَسَلَ فَالْغُسْلُ أَفْضَلُ - Tirmidhī, *k. al-jumuʿah b. mā jā' fī al-wuḍū' yawm al-jumuʿah*, 497 and Abū Dāwūd, *k. al-ṭahārah b. fī al-rukhṣah fī tark al-ghusl yawm al-jumuʿah*, 354

as well as constantly encouraging his Companions رضي الله عنهم to do so. Some jurists also refer to this as Sunnah al-Hudā (سُنَّةُ الْهُدَى). These are the actions, statements, and approvals of the Prophet ﷺ related to religious practices or actions that carry direct religious significance. For example, praying in congregation, the adhān, and select prayers before or after the obligatory prayers.[21] If a person does an act that is classified as sunnah mu'akkadah they will be rewarded. There is no sin or blame for choosing not to. However, it can become blameworthy if left out both consistently and intentionally. If a person consistently and intentionally leaves something that is considered to be sunnah mu'akkadah it is considered "turning away" from the Sunnah, which is blameworthy.

2. AL-SUNNAH GHAYR AL-MU'AKKADAH (السُّنَّةُ غَيرُ الْمُؤَكَّدَةِ): NON-EMPHASIZED SUNNAH

A non-emphasized sunnah is something the Prophet ﷺ did sometimes and at other times chose not to or did regularly, but didn't make it a point to constantly encourage his Companions رضي الله عنهم to do consistently. This type of act is also known as nafl or mustaḥab. For example, the four units of prayer before 'Ishā', fasting on Mondays and Thursdays, facing the qiblah when performing wuḍū', remaining quiet while listening to the adhān, replying to the adhān, and using and beginning with the right side for things that are considered good. A person who does something that is classified as a non-emphasized sunnah will be rewarded and there is no sin for choosing not to. However, by leaving it a person will be depriving themselves of a lot of good and reward.

An act that is considered to be a non-emphasized sunnah can also be part of sunnah al-hudā; meaning, it can be related to a religious practice or an act of worship. It can also be something that the scholars classify as Sunnah al-Zā'idah (سُنَّةُ الزَّائِدَةِ), or extra Sunnahs. These are ordinary daily tasks the Prophet ﷺ did as a human being such as the way he dressed, ate food, drank, the types of food he liked and disliked, the way he walked, and the way he slept. A person who chooses to act upon them seeking to follow the example of the Prophet ﷺ out of love, reverence, and respect will definitely be rewarded. At the same time there is absolutely no blame on a person who

---

21 These are the two before Fajr, 4 before Ẓuhr, 2 after Ẓuhr, 2 after Maghrib, and 2 after 'Ishā'. - Muslim, 728

chooses not to.

AL-HARAM (الحَرَامُ): **PROHIBITED**

Something that is ḥarām is defined as,

هُوَ مَا طَلَبَ الشَّارِعُ تَركَهُ عَلَى وَجهِ الحَتمِ وَالإِلزَامِ

An act that has been prohibited by the Lawgiver in certain and binding terms.

The Aḥnāf add to the definition that the prohibition has to be from a definitive proof. If it is from a speculative proof then the act is considered to be makrūh taḥrīman (prohibitively disliked). The certain and binding terms are understood from the syntax, context, grammar, or external evidence. For example, murder, theft, consuming intoxicants, and false accusations are all ḥarām.

Allah ﷻ prohibits interest in Sūrah al-Baqarah, "But Allah has permitted trade and has forbidden interest (ribā)."[22] The prohibition of unlawful intercourse (zinā) is mentioned in Sūrah al-Isrāʾ, "And do not even approach unlawful sexual intercourse (zinā). It is completely immoral, and wicked in nature."[23] Allah ﷻ also forbids the taking of false oaths as is mentioned in Sūrah al-Ḥajj "and refuse making false statements."[24]

An individual who does something that is prohibited is liable and deserving of blame and sin, but at the same time, will be rewarded for not committing those actions. According to the Aḥnāf a person who knowingly denies the prohibition of something that is ḥarām is considered to be out of the fold of Islam.

---

22 2:275

23 17:32

24 22:30

AL-MAKRUH (المَكرُوهُ): **DISLIKED**

Something that is makrūh is defined as,

هُوَ مَا طَلَبَ الشَّارِعُ تَرْكَهُ لَا عَلَى وَجهِ الحَتمِ وِالإِزلَامِ

An act that has been prohibited by the Lawgiver in non-binding terms.

The non-binding terms of the prohibition are understood through the syntax, grammar, or context of the prohibition itself as well as through external evidence. For example the Prophet ﷺ said, "Truly Allah has prohibited the disobedience of mothers, burying daughters alive, and withholding while asking. And He has disliked three things for you: vain talk about others ("he said she said"), excessive pointless questioning, and wasting wealth".[25] The distinction in wording of prohibition from "ḥarrama" and dislike from "kariha" is clear.

A person who intentionally leaves something that is disliked will be rewarded. There is no sin for choosing to do something that is disliked.

The Aḥnāf (Ḥanafīs), looking at both the theological and practical aspect of the ruling, divide something that is makrūh into two categories:

1. *AL-MAKRŪH TANZĪHAN* (المَكرُوهُ تَنْزِيها)*: SOMEWHAT DISLIKED*

Something that is somewhat disliked is defined as an act the Sharīʿah disapproves of without assigning any punishment or blame for one who does it. This is the exact same definition as something that is classified as makrūh according to the majority. For example, using too much water or too little water for wuḍūʾ, or not mentioning the name of Allah at the beginning of wuḍūʾ.[26]

A person who does something that is classified as somewhat disliked will not be considered sinful or blameworthy; however, they will be rewarded for leaving it intentionally.

25 إِنَّ اللَّهَ حَرَّمَ عَلَيْكُمْ عُقُوقَ الْأُمَّهَاتِ وَوَأْدَ الْبَنَاتِ وَمَنَعَ وَهَاتِ وَكَرِهَ لَكُمْ قِيلَ وَقَالَ وَكَثْرَةَ السُّؤَالِ وَإِضَاعَةَ الْمَالِ - Bukhārī, *k. fī al-istiqrāḍ, b. mā yunhā ʿan iḍāʿah al-māl*, 2408, *and k. al-adab, b. ʿuqūq al-wālidayn min al-kabāʾir*, 5975, Muslim, 4257 and 4260

26 This is the position within the Ḥanafī School of Thought.

2. AL-MAKRŪH TAḤRĪMAN (المَكرُوهُ تَحْرِيماً): PROHIBITIVELY DISLIKED

Something that is classified as prohibitively disliked is defined as an act prohibited by the Sharīʿah through a speculative text. It is an act that has been prohibited by the Lawgiver in certain and binding terms through a speculative text. For example, delaying ʿAṣr until the sun changes color, kissing one's spouse while fasting, and using gold and silver utensils.

A person who intentionally stays away from something that is prohibitively disliked will be rewarded, and if they choose to do it they will be liable and deserving of sin and punishment. With respect to the theological aspect of the ruling, a person who denies that the act is prohibitively disliked will not be out of the fold of Islam.

AL-MUBAH (المُبَاحُ): **PERMISSIBLE**

Something that is mubāḥ is defined as,

هُوَ مَا خَيَّرَ الشَّارِعُ المُكَلَّفَ فِيهِ بَيْنَ فِعلِهِ وَتَركِهِ

An act that the Lawgiver has neither commanded nor prohibited.

In other words, a person has the choice to do it or not. It is an act that is neither required nor prohibited by the Sharīʿah. Permissibility is often expressed using the expressions, "there is no harm for you" or "it is not a sin for you". For example, eating, drinking, sleeping, buying and selling etc.

When a person does something that is classified as mubāḥ, there is no reward and no sin. However, if done with a proper intention it can be transformed into an act of worship that is deserving of reward. Likewise, if done with an evil intention, one can be liable and deserving of punishment and sin.

AL-HUKM AL-WAD'IY (الحُكمُ الوَضعِيُّ) AND ITS TYPES

As mentioned earlier, al-ḥukm al-waḍʿiy is usually translated as

Declaratory Law. It is defined as a communication from Allah ﷻ that enacts something into a cause, condition, or a hindrance to something else. It is a ḥukm that declares the legal relationship between the cause (sabab) and its effect (musabbab) or between the precondition (sharṭ) and its object (mashrūṭ).

This type of legal rule does not create an obligation. It is a rule that facilitates or explains how a defining law functions or it explains the relationship between defining laws.

The scholars of Uṣūl classify declaratory law into five major categories:

1. sabab (cause)
2. sharṭ (precondition)
3. māniʿ (hindrance)
4. ṣaḥiḥ (valid) and bāṭil (invalid)
5. ʿazīmah (base standard) and rukhṣah (concession)

AS-SABAB (السَّبَبُ) WA AL-SHART WA AL-MANI' (المَانِعُ): THE CAUSE, PRECONDITION AND HINDRANCE

These are rules that are either causes of, conditions for, or obstacles to a legal ruling.

SABAB (سَبَبٌ): CAUSE

The word sabab literally refers to the means to a thing. For example, reading is a means to gaining knowledge. Technically, according to the scholars of Uṣūl, a sabab is the cause on the basis of which a rule is established. If the sabab exists, then the defined law exists and if the sabab doesn't exist then the defined law won't exist.

هُوَ مَا يَلزَمُ مِن وُجُودِهِ الوُجُودُ وَمِن عَدَمِهِ العَدَمُ

It is the incident whose existence is the prerequisite for the existence of the ruling and its absence is an indication of the absence of the ruling.

For example, time is the cause of prayer, the month of Ramaḍān is the cause for fasting, travel is the cause for the permissibility of not fasting, and a sale is the cause of ownership.

SHARṬ (شَرطٌ): PRECONDITION

A sharṭ is defined as something upon which the existence of another thing depends, but its existence does not necessarily mean the existence of that thing. Technically, it is an evident and constant attribute whose absence necessitates the absence of the ḥukm but whose presence does not automatically bring about its object.

هُوَ مَا يَلزَمُ مِن عَدَمِهِ العَدَمُ وَلَا يَلزَمُ مِن وُجُودِهِ وُجُودٌ وَلَا عَدَمٌ

It is something that is needed for the ruling or act to exist, but if it's there it doesn't necessarily mean the ruling or act will be there.

Examples:

1. Purity is a precondition for the validity of prayer.
2. Two witnesses are a precondition for marriage.
3. Passing of a year is a precondition for the obligation of zakāh.
4. Being married is a precondition for divorce to be valid.

AL-MĀNIʿ (المَانِعُ): HINDRANCE

A mānīʿ is,

هُوَ مَا يَلزَمُ مِن وُجُودِهِ العَدَمُ وَلَا يَلزَمُ مِن عَدَمِهِ وُجُودٌ وَلَا عَدَمٌ

Something whose existence necessitates the absence of the ḥukm or nullifies the cause of the ḥukm.

A condition or a set of facts may exist that prevent the ḥukm from being applied, even if the cause is found and the condition is met. A mānīʿ is something whose existence necessitates the absence of the ḥukm or its sabab. If there's a mānīʿ, there's no ḥukm.

For example, difference of religion is a hindrance to inheritance between a legal heir and their deceased relative. Even though there is a valid tie of kinship between the two individuals they still won't inherit because of the mānī'. Another example is doubt in the cases of prescribed punishments (ḥudūd). Even the slightest amount of doubt prevents a prescribed punishment such as the punishment for unlawful sexual intercourse from being carried out.

AL-SAHIH (الصَحِيحُ) WA AL-BATIL (البَاطِلُ): **VALID AND INVALID**

Something that is classified as wājib, mandūb, or mubāḥ may be required to be performed in a certain way by the Lawgiver. An act is classified as ṣaḥīḥ (valid) when something is done fulfilling all of its preconditions and integrals.

مَا يَتَعَلَّقُ بِهِ النُفُوذُ وَيُعتَدُّ بِهِ عِبَادَةً كَانَت أَو مُعَامَلَة

That which is effective, takes place, and is given valid legal consideration -- both acts of worship and transactions.

When something is done without fulfilling all of its preconditions and integrals it is classified as bāṭil (invalid). Meaning, one of the preconditions or integrals of the act is missing.

مَا لَا يَتَعَلَّقُ بِهِ النُفُوذُ وَلَا يُعتَدُّ بِهِ عِبَادَةً كَانَت أَو مُعَامَلَةً

That which is ineffective, does not take place, and is not given valid legal consideration -- both acts of worship and transactions.

For example, if a person prays fulfilling all of its preconditions, integrals, wājibāt, sunan, and etiquettes then it will be classified as being valid. However, if a person prays without reciting the Quran, or without prostrating, or without purity, the prayer will be invalid. Similarly, if a person fasts while fulfilling all of its preconditions and integrals it will be classified as being valid. However, if they intentionally eat while fasting it will become invalid.

The classification of acts into valid and invalid can actually be thought of as legal values that describe and evaluate legal acts that are performed. All of the scholars agree that acts of worship (ʿibādāt) are either valid or invalid, there's no middle ground. The majority of scholars maintain a similar view regarding transactions; a transaction can either be valid or invalid; there is nothing in between. Only a valid contract gives rise to its legal consequences, which is transfer of ownership.

The Aḥnāf and others add another intermediary category: those transactions that are fāsid (corrupt). When the deficiency in the contract affects an integral, meaning an intrinsic part of the contract, then the contract will be null and void. If, however, the deficiency affects a condition or something extrinsic to the actual contract, it will be fāsid, not bāṭil. A fāsid contract, although deficient in some respects, is still a valid contract and some of its legal consequences take effect, such as ownership.

According to the Aḥnāf, something that is fāsid is still lawful but is deficient in respect to an attribute (waṣf) as opposed to something that is bāṭil, which is considered unlawful. This difference is rooted in the idea that the deficiency that affects the attribute but not the essence of a transaction can often be removed and rectified. For example, if a contract of sale is concluded without specifying the price, it's possible to do so afterwards and rectify it.

AL-ʿAZIMAH (العَزِيمَة) WA AL-RUKHSAH (الرُّخصَة): **ORIGINAL LAW AND CONCESSION**

According to the scholars of Uṣūl, an ʿazīmah is a legal ruling that was legislated initially as a general rule under normal circumstances and conditions. It's the law as the Lawgiver intended it to be; the law in its normal and original state. For example, praying the prayers in full, fasting, paying zakāh, and performing ḥajj under normal and regular circumstances. An ʿazīmah can either be wājib, mandūb, ḥarām, makrūh, or mubāḥ.

A rukhṣah, on the other hand, is an exemption or a concession from the original rule. It is a ruling that comes into play because of valid excuses such as difficulty, necessity, and duress. An ʿazīmah is the law in its normal state and a rukhṣah is the exception the Lawgiver has granted to facilitate ease in difficult circumstances. The two are interrelated since a rukhṣah can only exist when there's an ʿazīmah in the first place.

For example, the law that grants travellers an exemption from fasting is a considered a rukhṣah. Similarly, drinking wine and other intoxicants is prohibited as a general rule. However, in cases of duress, one is allowed to consume wine or other intoxicants if it saves them from dying of thirst. Eating the flesh of a carcass is also prohibited. However, in cases of duress one is allowed to consume it, if it saves them from dying of starvation. Another example of a rukhṣah is shortening prayer because of travelling.

A rukhṣah is of three types:

1. Permitting a prohibited act because of necessity or hardship

   For example, professing disbelief under coercion, threat of torture or death — as long as faith is still firm in one's heart — to save one's life.
2. Permissibility of leaving something that's wājib because of difficulty

   For example, the permissibility of not fasting if a person is travelling or sick. As Allah ﷻ says, "So whoever among you is ill or on a journey [during those days] - then an equal number of days [are to be made up]."[27]
3. The permissibility of certain contracts that are normally not allowed because of necessity or custom

   For example, selling something that doesn't exist is usually not permissible. However, an advance sale (salam) and order for manufactured goods (istiṣnā') are allowed because of the public need for these types of transactions.

---

27 2:184

PART 2:

SOURCES OF ISLAMIC LAW

4

AL-ADILLATU ASH-SHAR'IYYAH:

SOURCES OF ISLAMIC LAW

Within the Sharīʿah there are certain proofs or sources that are used to derive Islamic Law. Put simply, legal rulings (aḥkām) are derived from proofs (adillah). The word adillah is the plural of the word dalīl, which literally means guide, proof, indication, or evidence. Technically, a dalīl is defined as an indication in the sources from which a practical legal ruling (ḥukm) is derived. In the terminology of the Scholars of Uṣūl it refers to the proofs or sources of the Sharīʿah.

PRIMARY AND SECONDARY

Depending on how a scholar is viewing the evidences, they can be categorized in several different ways. One of the ways of classifying them is into primary and secondary sources. The primary sources are those that are unanimously agreed upon by the four schools of thought:

1. Quran
2. Sunnah
3. Ijmāʿ
4. Qiyās

The secondary sources are those that are not unanimously accepted by the four schools of thought. The most well-known are:

1. al-Istiḥsān (Juristic Preference)
2. al-Maṣlaḥah al-Mursalah (Public Interest)
3. al-Istiṣḥāb (Presumption of Continuity)
4. al-ʿUrf (Custom)
5. Madhab al-Ṣahābī (Opinion of a Companion)
6. Sharʿ man Qablana (Laws of those before us)
7. Sad al-Dharīʿah (Blocking the Means)

DEFINITIVE AND SPECULATIVE

Another way to classify evidence is into:

1. Definitive (قَطعِيٌّ)
2. Speculative (ظَنِّيٌّ)

There are two aspects to every dalīl:

1. authenticity (thubūt)
2. meaning (dalālah)

Both the authenticity and the meaning can be definitive or speculative. There are four possible combinations, one of them is referred to as a definitive proof and the other three as speculative.

If both the authenticity and meaning are definite, then the dalīl is classified as definitive. As for a speculative proof, then it can be definitive in terms of authenticity and speculative in terms of meaning, speculative in terms of authenticity and definitive in terms of meaning, or speculative in terms of both authenticity and meaning.

TRANSMITTED AND RATIONAL

Another way of classifying evidences is into transmitted (نَقلِيٌّ) and rational (عَقلِيٌّ). Transmitted proofs are those that have come to us through various channels of transmission. For example, the Quran, Sunnah, and Ijmāʿ. These proofs are independent of rational justification, although most of them can also be justified rationally. Rational proofs, on the other hand, are founded in reason and need to be rationally justified. For example, Qiyās, Istiḥsān, Istiṣlāḥ, and Istiṣḥāb (all to be discussed later) are all classified as rational proofs although they are dependent upon transmitted proofs.

An extremely important point to always keep in mind is that rationality alone is not an independent proof in Islam. For example, Qiyās is a rational proof, but in order for it to be valid, it has to be based on an established ruling from the Quran or Sunnah.

ORDER OF PRIORITY FOR THE SOURCES

There is an established order of priority between the sources of Law. When searching for a legal ruling, scholars follow an established and set methodology. When searching for the ruling of a particular issue, jurists will first approach the Quran. If they can't find it in the Quran, they turn to the Sunnah of the Prophet ﷺ. If they can't find the answer in the Sunnah of the Prophet ﷺ, then they turn to the consensus of the scholars. If they can't find any consensus on the issue then they turn to Qiyās.

There are a number of verses in the Quran and narrations from the Prophet ﷺ that identify the sources of the Sharīʿah and the order of priority between them. For example, Allah ﷻ says in Sūrah al-Nisāʾ, "O you who have believed, obey Allah and obey the Messenger and those in authority among you. And if you disagree over anything, refer it to Allah and the Messenger, if you should believe in Allah and the Last Day. That is the best [way] and best in result."[28] The commentators mention that "obey Allah" refers to the Quran, "obey the Messenger" refers to the Sunnah, "obey those in authority among you" refers to having recourse to ijmāʿ, and "if you disagree over anything, refer it to Allah and the Messenger" refers to Qiyās.

Another proof for this particular methodology is the well-known ḥadīth of Muʿādh ibn Jabal رضي الله عنه. When the Messenger of Allah ﷺ sent Muʿādh ibn Jabal to Yemen he asked, "How will you judge when the occasion of deciding a case arises?" He replied, "I will judge according to the book of Allah." He asked, "And if you don't find it in the book of Allah?" He replied, "Then I'll

28 4:59

judge according to the Sunnah of the Messenger of Allah." He asked, "And if you don't find it in the Sunnah of the Messenger of Allah?" He replied, "I'll do ijtihād (my best to form an opinion) and spare no pains." The Prophet ﷺ then patted him on the chest and said, "Praise be to Allah who helped the messenger of the Messenger of Allah to find that which pleases the Messenger of Allah."[29] This ḥadīth highlights the order in which the sources are supposed to be approached. This is the exact methodology that was adopted by the Companions of the Prophet ﷺ. For example, this methodology was adopted by Abū Bakr ؓ and ʿUmar ؓ as mentioned earlier on pages 11 and 12. Something similar is also narrated from several other companions such as ibn Masʿūd ؓ. This is the exact same methodology used by jurists today.

29 Abū Dāwūd, k. *al-aqḍiyah*, b. *ijtihād al-ra'y fī al-qaḍā'*, 3592

5

AL-QURAN

In order to get a feeling for the greatness of the Quran it is enough to say that it is the divine uncreated speech of Allah ﷻ, the Creator of the Heavens and the Earth and everything they contain. It is the last and final revelation sent for the guidance of humanity until the end of times. Its words are so powerful, emotive, and effective that if they were to be revealed on a mountain, it would be humbled and burst apart out of the awe of Allah ﷻ.[30] Its recitation, memorization, interpretation, understanding, teaching, and learning are all acts of worship that bring blessings and reward. These words are a source of light, guidance, cure, and mercy.

Since the time of the Quran's revelation until today, the Muslim community has served the Book of Allah ﷻ in numerous ways, leaving behind a very rich and exhaustive tradition. But none can ever claim to have done complete justice to the Book; it remains an ocean that calls devotees of every era to dive into its depths to extract new pearls and treasures. There are many descriptions of the Quran written by great linguists and poets, but there is none more eloquent than the description of the Prophet ﷺ himself. The Prophet ﷺ said, "Allah's book. In it is news of those before you, information about what comes after you, and judgment for what happens between you. It is the Criterion (between right and wrong) without jest. Whoever among

30 59:21

the oppressors abandons it, Allah crushes him, and whoever seeks guidance from other than it, then Allah leaves him to stray. It is the firm rope of Allah, the wise remembrance, the straight path. It is the one that desires cannot distort, nor can the tongues twist, nor can the scholars ever have enough of it. It shall not become dull from repetition, and the wonders of it do not diminish. It is the one that when the Jinns heard it, they did not hesitate to say about it: 'Verily, we have heard a wonderful Recitation (this Quran)! It guides to the Right Path, and we have believed.' Whoever speaks according to it has spoken the truth; whoever acts according to it is rewarded; whoever judges by it has been just, and whoever invites to it has been guided to the straight path."[31]

When talking about definitions, scholars talk about the linguistic as well as the technical meaning of a word. Words have linguistic definitions but often times because of coinage, usage, custom, and other factors, they take on different meanings.

Linguistically, the word Quran is derived from the root verb qara'a (قرأ) which means to read or to recite. So the word Quran is the verbal noun, which means the reading or the recitation. The word Quran literally means the reading, the recitation, or that which is read or recited. One of the reasons why it has been named the Quran is because it is a book that is recited by Muslims throughout the world and will continue to be recited until the end of times.

Scholars are very precise when defining terms by using exact language and carefully choosing words. A good definition has to be both inclusive and exclusive; inclusive means that it has to include everything that is essential to the term being defined and exclusive means that it has to exclude everything that is extraneous to the term.

The agreed upon definition of the Quran is that it is the inimitable Arabic speech of Allah ﷻ that He revealed to Muḥammad ﷺ through the Angel Jibrīl ﷺ, which has been preserved in the maṣāḥif (written copies of the Quran), and has reached us by mutawātir transmission.

The first part of the definition, "the inimitable Arabic…," establishes two things: the miraculous nature of the Quran and that the Quran is in the Arabic language. Part of the miracle of the Quran is that no one can produce anything similar to it. By mentioning that the Quran is in Arabic, all

31 al-Tirmidhī, *k. faḍā'il Al-Qur'ān 'an rasūl Allāh*, 3153

translations of the text are excluded from the definition.

The second part of the definition states that the Quran is the "speech of Allah" This excludes the speech of any other creation, which includes the statements of the Prophet ﷺ. The Quran is the speech of Allah ﷻ that He spoke in a manner that is befitting to Him. That is why the ḥadīth are not considered to be Quran.

The third part of the definition, "that He revealed to Muḥammad ﷺ" excludes revelation sent to the previous Prophets such as Mūsā عليه السلام and ʿĪsā عليه السلام.

The fourth part of the definition, "through the Angel Jibrīl عليه السلام" limits the Quran to revelation the Prophet ﷺ received through Jibrīl. There were other ways the Prophet ﷺ received revelation as well, such as dreams.

The fifth part of the definition, "which has been preserved in the maṣāḥif," refers to the copies of the Quran that were written during the time of Abū Bakr رضي الله عنه and ʿUthmān رضي الله عنه and were distributed throughout the Muslim world.

The last part of the definition, "and has reached us by mutawātir transmission," explains how the Quran has reached us from the time of the Prophet ﷺ. A report is considered to be mutawātir when it is transmitted by such a large number of people in each generation so that it is impossible for them to have agreed upon a lie either intentionally or unintentionally. So many people transmitted it that it is impossible for it to be a forgery. Something that is transmitted through tawātur gives the benefit of certainty.

This is the technical definition formulated by the scholars of uṣūl and fiqh. The purpose of this definition is to simply identify what is meant by the word "Quran" and not to capture the actual essence of the Quran. Beyond this definition, and perhaps more important, is to understand that the Quran is a book of guidance. Everything that is mentioned in the Quran is done so for the guidance of humanity. The stories and parables, commands and prohibitions, signs in the universe and the human body, and everything else mentioned is for guidance. Allah ﷻ Himself describes the Quran as "guidance for humanity."[32] It provides guidance for every single aspect of human life.

32 2:185

AUTHORITY

For Muslims as people of faith, the authority of the Quran is apparent and clear; it really doesn't need any explanation. The Quran is the divine, eternal, uncreated speech of Allah ﷻ, the Lord, the Creator of the heavens and the earth and everything they contain, the Sustainer, the Nourisher, the One who gives life and the One who gives death. The authority of the Quran comes directly from Allah ﷻ. Muslims believe with absolute certainty that the Quran is the speech of Allah ﷻ in both words and meanings. It is the primary source of faith, religion, and its teachings.

Another aspect that allows humans to recognize the authority of the Quran is the miraculous nature of the Quran itself, which is referred to as Iʿjāz al-Quran. Iʿjāz al-Quran refers to the concept that the Quran is inimitable; nothing remotely similar to it can be produced or composed. Iʿjāz highlights the inability of humans, angels, and jinns, both individually and collectively, to imitate or produce something similar to the Quran. The Quran is distinct and unique; it can't be rivaled or imitated.

The Quran was a challenge, specifically to the Arabs, and to all of humanity. The Prophet ﷺ was ordered by Allah ﷻ to challenge those who rejected the message to produce something similar to the Quran. The non-believers had a reason to accept this challenge and there was nothing preventing them from doing so. And this challenge was posed at the hands of an unlettered Prophet ﷺ who didn't know how to read or write. He didn't study at any school or university nor did he learn sciences or arts from any scholar. Despite all of this, not one person accepted this challenge.

The purpose of this challenge is to show that the Quran is divine, miraculous, and that it is without a doubt the absolute truth, and that the Prophet ﷺ is truthful in what he claimed. And this helps humans understand the authority of the Quran.

LEGAL RULINGS IN THE QURAN

In Surah Yūsuf, Allah ﷻ describes the Quran as, "Never was the Quran an invented narration, but rather, it's a confirmation of what was before it and a detailed explanation of all things and guidance and mercy for a people who believe."[33] The Quran confirms and reaffirms what is mentioned in the scriptures that came before it. Allah ﷻ Himself says that the Quran is a detailed explanation of every single thing. Ibn Masʿūd ؓ said, "Whoever wants knowledge then let them turn to the Quran." Imām al-Shāfiʿī said, "Nothing happens to anyone with respect to their religion except that there is guidance for it in the book of Allah." Once he said, "Ask me about anything and I will tell you about it from the book of Allah." That is why Ibn ʿAbbās ؓ would say that if he lost his camel's rope, he would find it in the book of Allah. Meaning that he would look towards the Quran for answers to all of his problems, both big and small.

The primary objective of the Quran is to teach and remind humanity about certain absolute truths and realities that form part of the system of belief of Islam. It explains the relationship between humanity and their Creator. The second objective is to detail the rules and regulations that govern everyday life. It provides guidance for life as an individual, as a member of a family, and as a member of society. It provides guidance with respect to social, economic, religious, and political life.

The Quran talks about beliefs, law, history, and parables. It even contains knowledge that is associated with the fields of medicine, debate, astronomy, engineering, algebra, and geology. Although the Quran contains knowledge regarding these sciences and many others, it is not a book of history, science, or medicine. It is a book of guidance. That is why the verses of the Quran discuss four major topics:

1. beliefs
2. stories
3. parables
4. legal rulings and commandments

Since the focus of this introductory book is on the methodology of Law, the discussion here will be limited to the verses related to legal rulings and commandments.

33 12:111

AYAT AL-AHKAM (آيَاتُ الأَحكَام): **LEGAL VERSES**

The Quran can be thought of as a guidebook for life, the instruction manual given to humanity in order to teach them how to live life according to the rule of God. In this context, the Quran is a book of law containing both commandments and prohibitions. The verses that talk about law are known as Āyāt al-Aḥkām — legal verses. There are approximately three hundred and fifty verses that deal with laws out of the nearly seven thousand verses. The commandments found in the Quran can be divided into two broad categories: ritual or devotional matters (ʿibādāt) and civil or contractual transactions (muʿāmalāt). Devotional matters are rules that regulate the relationship between individual and Creator, and civil transactions are concerned with humans and humanity.

There are verses that give basic guidelines for devotional matters such as purification, prayer, fasting, charity, ḥajj, and sacrifice. These are also classified as the rights of Allah ﷻ. The detailed rulings for these acts of worship are found in the Sunnah of the Prophet ﷺ.

The verses talking about civil transactions discuss a wide range of subjects including marriage, divorce, paternity, inheritance, and family-law. There are commandments applying to facets of commercial law such as sale, lease, and loan. There are verses that address issues related to criminal law such as murder, highway robbery, theft, drinking, adultery, and slanderous accusation. Other verses deal with matters related to civil law: justice, equality, evidence, consultation, personal rights, and freedoms.

Although the Quran does contain some detailed legal rulings, most legal verses deal with broader principles and concepts. These verses provide general guidelines on every topic of Islamic Law. The details then come in the form of the actions, statements, and tacit approvals of the Prophet ﷺ.

Again, it is important to remember that the Quran is not a legal document even though it contains laws. The vast majority of verses deal with morality, guidance, and theology. The Quran contains verses that regulate social behavior by encouraging kindness, sympathy, compassion, care, forgiveness, love, mercy, patience, forbearance, steadfastness, courage, and generosity. Therefore, the Quran provides a complete moral, ethical, and legal code for life.

6

THE SUNNAH

The second most important source of Islamic Law is the Sunnah of the Prophet ﷺ. Linguistically speaking, the word sunnah conveys the meaning of,

السِّيرَةُ وَالطَّرِيقَةُ المُعتَادَةُ حَسَنَةً كَانَت أَو قَبِيحَةً

A way or usual path, regardless of whether it is good or bad.

Technically, the word sunnah can have different meanings depending on who is using it and in what context it is being used. In the most general sense, it refers to the way of the Prophet ﷺ in everything he did, regardless of whether that action is legally considered to be obligatory (farḍ), mandatory (wājib), or recommended (mustaḥabb).

الطَّرِيقَةُ المَشْرُوعَةُ المُتَّبَعَةُ فِي الدِّينِ وَالمَنهَجُ النَّبَوِيُّ الحَنِيفُ

The legally observed way in the religion and in the orthodox prophetic practice.

According to the jurists, it is a legal value assigned to a person's actions.

If a person does it, then they will be rewarded. If they leave it, then there is no blame upon them. The jurists define it as,

مَا وَاظَبَ عَلَيهِ النَّبِيُ ﷺ عَلَى وَجهِ العِبَادَةِ مَعَ التَّركِ أَحيَانًا لِغَيرِ عُذرٍ

Something that the Prophet ﷺ did on a regular and consistent basis as an act of devotion, while leaving it sometimes without an excuse.

As for the scholars of ḥadīth, they use it as a synonym for the word ḥadīth.

Within the scope of Uṣūl al-Fiqh, Sunnah refers to the statements, actions, or tacit approvals attributed to the Prophet ﷺ. The Sunnah of the Prophet ﷺ is captured in aḥadīth, narrations or reports, that describe the statements, actions, and tacit approvals of the Prophet ﷺ.

AUTHORITY AND IMPORTANCE OF THE SUNNAH

The importance of aḥadīth and the Sunnah within the framework of Islam cannot be overemphasized; they are a foundational aspect of our belief and practice. There are two primary sources of Islam: the Quran and Sunnah. Broadly speaking, the Quran provides us with general rules, principles, morals, values, ethics, and ideals while the Sunnah provides the details. The Sunnah of the Prophet ﷺ is a detailed explanation of what is mentioned by Allah ﷻ in the Quran. It is impossible to act upon the Quran, to follow its guidance, teachings, commands, and prohibitions without the Sunnah of the Prophet ﷺ. There are a number of reasons why the Sunnah is considered to be central to Islamic beliefs and practices and several articles and booklets have been written on this topic.

It is narrated that once ʿImrān ibn Ḥuṣayn رضي الله عنه was sitting with his students when a man came and said, "Do not speak to us except with the Quran." ʿImrān asked him to come close and said, "Tell me, if you and your companions relied upon the Quran alone, would you find that ẓuhr prayer is four units, ʿaṣr is four units, maghrib is three units, and that you have to recite in the first two units? Tell me, if you and your companions relied upon the Quran alone, would you find that ṭawāf is seven circuits and that walking between Ṣafā and Marwah is seven circuits? O people! Take the Sunnah from us, because, by Allah, if you do not, you will go astray."[34]

This incident highlights just one aspect of the importance of the Sunnah. Without it, we would have no practical way of implementing the Quran. We would not know how to worship Allah ﷻ properly. Imām Abū Ḥanīfah ﵀ said, "Had it not been for the Sunnah, none of us would have understood the Quran." Imām al-Shāfiʿī ﵀ said, "Everything the imāms say is an explanation of the Sunnah, and the entire Sunnah is an explanation of the Quran."

EXPLAINING THE QURAN

Allah ﷻ revealed the noble Quran as a book of guidance illuminating the path towards happiness and success both in this world and the next. Allah ﷻ gave the Quran to the Prophet ﷺ as an everlasting miracle, whose miraculous nature can be seen and experienced till the end of time. Along with the Quran, Allah ﷻ gave the Prophet ﷺ the Sunnah as a detailed explanation of what is in the Quran.

Allah ﷻ says,

وَأَنزَلْنَا إِلَيْكَ الذِّكْرَ لِتُبَيِّنَ لِلنَّاسِ مَا نُزِّلَ إِلَيْهِمْ وَلَعَلَّهُمْ يَتَفَكَّرُونَ

We revealed the message to you so you can explain to people what was sent down to them and then they might give it some thought.[35]

Allah ﷻ also says,

وَمَا أَنزَلْنَا عَلَيْكَ الْكِتَابَ إِلَّا لِتُبَيِّنَ لَهُمُ الَّذِى اخْتَلَفُوا فِيهِ ۙ وَهُدًى وَرَحْمَةً لِّقَوْمٍ يُؤْمِنُونَ

And We have not revealed to you the Book, [O Muḥammad], except for you to make clear to them what they have differed about, and as a

34 al-Bayhaqī, *madkhal al-dalāʾil*, 1:25

35 16:44

guidance and mercy for those who believe.[36]

In these two verses and several others throughout the Quran, Allah ﷻ is explicitly stating that one of the responsibilities of the Prophet ﷺ is to explain the Book of Allah ﷻ. The Sunnah of the Prophet ﷺ is a detailed explanation of what is mentioned by Allah ﷻ in the Quran. It is impossible to act upon the Quran, to follow its guidance, teachings, commands, and prohibitions without the Sunnah of the Prophet ﷺ.

OBLIGATION TO FOLLOW THE SUNNAH

In addition to that, there are numerous verses that make it explicitly clear that it is obligatory to follow the Sunnah of the Prophet ﷺ. In several places throughout the Quran, Allah ﷻ makes it an obligation upon believers to obey and follow His messenger. Take the following examples:

يَا أَيُّهَا الَّذِينَ آمَنُوا أَطِيعُوا اللَّهَ وَأَطِيعُوا الرَّسُولَ وَأُولِي الْأَمْرِ مِنكُمْ ۖ
فَإِن تَنَازَعْتُمْ فِي شَيْءٍ فَرُدُّوهُ إِلَى اللَّهِ وَالرَّسُولِ إِن كُنتُمْ تُؤْمِنُونَ
بِاللَّهِ وَالْيَوْمِ الْآخِرِ ۚ ذَٰلِكَ خَيْرٌ وَأَحْسَنُ تَأْوِيلًا

O you who have believed, obey Allah and obey the Messenger and those in authority among you. And if you disagree over anything, refer it back to Allah and the Messenger, if you believe in Allah and the Last Day. That is the best [way] and best in result.[37]

مَّن يُطِعِ الرَّسُولَ فَقَدْ أَطَاعَ اللَّهَ

Whoever obeys the Messenger has obeyed Allah.[38]

وَمَا كَانَ لِمُؤْمِنٍ وَلَا مُؤْمِنَةٍ إِذَا قَضَى اللَّهُ وَرَسُولُهُ أَمْرًا أَن يَكُونَ
لَهُمُ الْخِيَرَةُ مِنْ أَمْرِهِمْ ۗ وَمَن يَعْصِ اللَّهَ وَرَسُولَهُ فَقَدْ ضَلَّ ضَلَالًا

36 16:64
37 4:59
38 4:80

مُّبِينًا

It is not allowed for a believing man or believing woman, that, after Allah and His Messenger have decided a matter, that they should have any choice about their affair. And whoever disobeys Allah and His Messenger has certainly strayed into clear error.[39]

وَمَا آتَاكُمُ الرَّسُولُ فَخُذُوهُ وَمَا نَهَاكُمْ عَنْهُ فَانتَهُوا

And whatever the Messenger has given you - take it; and what he has forbidden you - stay away from it.[40]

قُلْ إِن كُنتُمْ تُحِبُّونَ اللَّهَ فَاتَّبِعُونِي يُحْبِبْكُمُ اللَّهُ وَيَغْفِرْ لَكُمْ ذُنُوبَكُمْ ۗ وَاللَّهُ غَفُورٌ رَّحِيمٌ

Say, [O Muḥammad], 'If you claim to love Allah, then follow me; Allah will love you and forgive your sins. Allah is Forgiving and Merciful.'[41]

The claim that following the Sunnah is not necessary or that the aḥadīth are *unreliable is absolutely ridiculous.*[42]

Similarly, there are a number of narrations from the Prophet ﷺ that talk about the importance of holding on to his guidance in every single situation, whether big or small, significant or insignificant. The Prophet ﷺ said,

لاَ أُلْفِيَنَّ أَحَدَكُمْ مُتَّكِئًا عَلَى أَرِيكَتِهِ يَأْتِيهِ الأَمْرُ مِنْ أَمْرِى مِمَّا أَمَرْتُ بِهِ أَوْ نَهَيْتُ عَنْهُ فَيَقُولُ لاَ نَدْرِى مَا وَجَدْنَا فِى كِتَابِ اللَّهِ اتَّبَعْنَاهُ

I hope I don't find any of you sitting on your couches when something I have spoken about [and made permissible or forbidden] is discussed, and

39 33:36

40 59:7

41 3:31

42 For more information, read *Introduction to Ūlūm al-Ḥadīth*

you say, 'Well, I don't know. We only follow what's in the Quran.'[43]

And he ﷺ said,

أَلاَ هَلْ عَسَى رَجُلٌ يَبْلُغُهُ الْحَدِيثُ عَنِّي وَهُوَ مُتَّكِئٌ عَلَى أَرِيكَتِهِ فَيَقُولُ بَيْنَنَا وَبَيْنَكُمْ كِتَابُ اللَّهِ فَمَا وَجَدْنَا فِيهِ حَلاَلاً اسْتَحْلَلْنَاهُ وَمَا وَجَدْنَا فِيهِ حَرَامًا حَرَّمْنَاهُ وَإِنَّ مَا حَرَّمَ رَسُولُ اللَّهِ صلى الله عليه وسلم كَمَا حَرَّمَ اللَّهُ

A time will come when someone comes to know of a narration of mine while sitting on his couch, and will respond by saying, 'We only rely on the Quran. Whatever is says is permissible, we consider permissible, and whatever it prohibits, we consider prohibited.' [Don't they know that] the verdicts and judgments of the Messenger of God is exactly like the judgment of God?[44]

And he ﷺ said,

فَعَلَيْكُمْ بِسُنَّتِي وَسُنَّةِ الْخُلَفَاءِ الرَّاشِدِينَ الْمَهْدِيِّينَ عَضُّوا عَلَيْهَا بِالنَّوَاجِذِ وَإِيَّاكُمْ وَمُحْدَثَاتِ الأُمُورِ۞ فَإِنَّ كُلَّ بِدْعَةٍ ضَلاَلَةٌ

You must follow my sunnah and the sunnah of the khulafāʾ al-rashidūn (the rightly guided caliphs), those who guide to the correct way. Cling to it stubbornly [literally: with your molar teeth]. Beware of newly invented matters [in the religion], for verily every innovation (bidʿah) is misguidance.[45]

And he ﷺ said,

أَمَّا بَعْدُ فَإِنَّ خَيْرَ الْحَدِيثِ كِتَابُ اللَّهِ وَخَيْرُ الْهُدَى هُدَى مُحَمَّدٍ

43 Abū Dāwūd, *k. al-sunnah, b. fī luzūm al-sunnah*, 4605, and Ibn Mājah, *muqaddimah*, 13

44 al-Tirmidhī, *k. al-ʿilm ʿan rasūlillāh* ﷺ, *b. mā nuhiy ʿanh an yuqāl ʿind ḥadīth al-nabī*, 2664, and Ibn Mājah, *muqaddimah*, 12

45 Ibid, 4607

صَلَّى اللَّهُ عَلَيهِ وَسَلَّمَ وَشَرُّ الأُمُورِ مُحْدَثَاتُهَا وَكُلُّ بِدْعَةٍ ضَلاَلَةٌ

To proceed, the best speech is the Book of Allah and the best guidance is the guidance of Muḥammad ﷺ, the worst practice is the introduction of new practices in Islam and every innovation (in religion) is misguidance.[46]

There are also multiple narrations that encourage believers to revive and follow the Sunnah of the Prophet ﷺ. These narrations outline the blessings, rewards, and virtues of following in the footsteps of the Prophet ﷺ. Take the following sayings for example:

The Prophet ﷺ said,

مَنْ أَحْيَا سُنَّةً مِنْ سُنَّتِي قَدْ أُمِيتَتْ بَعْدِى فَإِنَّ لَهُ مِنَ الأَجْرِ مِثْلَ أَجْرِ مَنْ عَمِلَ بِهَا مِنَ النَّاسِ لاَ يَنْقُصُ مِنْ أُجُورِ النَّاسِ شَيْئًا

Whoever revives a Sunnah of mine that has died out (become lost or abandoned) after I am gone will have a reward equivalent to everyone who then acts upon it, without that detracting from their reward in the slightest.[47]

The Prophet ﷺ also said,

المُستَمسِكُ بِسُنَّتِي عِندَ فَسَادِ أُمَّتِي لَهُ أَجرُ مِائَةِ شَهِيدٍ

The one who holds on tightly to my Sunnah when corruption in my nation spreads, for him the reward of a hundred martyrs.[48]

MODEL BEHAVIOR/ROLE MODEL

Allah ﷻ says,

46 Muslim, *k. al-jumuʿah, b. takhfīf al-ṣalah wa al-khuṭbah*, 867
47 Tirmidhī, *k. al-ʿilm ʿan rasūlillah* ﷺ, *b. mā jāʾa fī al-akdh bi al-sunnah wa ijtināb al-bidaʿi*, 2677
48 Haythamī, *majmaʿ al-zawāʾid*, 177

لَّقَدْ كَانَ لَكُمْ فِي رَسُولِ اللَّهِ أُسْوَةٌ حَسَنَةٌ لِّمَن كَانَ يَرْجُو اللَّهَ
وَالْيَوْمَ الْآخِرَ وَذَكَرَ اللَّهَ كَثِيرًا

Indeed in the Messenger of Allah you have a good example to follow for him who hopes in Allah and the Last Day and remembers Allah much.[49]

The Prophet ﷺ is the ideal role model for believers to follow in every single aspect of their lives; personal, social, communal, economic, and political. The Prophet ﷺ was a physical manifestation of the teachings of the Quran; his life was built upon the beliefs, morals, values, and principles mentioned in the Quran. That's why when his wife ʿĀ'ishah ؓ was asked regarding his character she replied, "His character was the Quran."[50] The Prophet ﷺ had the most noble character and manners; he was extremely kind, gentle, caring, friendly, affable, generous, compassionate, patient, forbearing, forgiving, brave, humble, and simple. He dealt with people in the most beautiful way possible. Allah ﷻ praises him in the Quran saying, "You truly possess the most excellent standard of character."[51]

That is why history has seen scholars of ḥadīth in every single generation striving, struggling, and putting a lot of importance in preserving and reviving the Sunnah of the Prophet ﷺ. It is through their tireless efforts that almost every single aspect of the life of the Prophet ﷺ has been preserved. This effort started with the companions of the Prophet ﷺ and continues till this day.

AHADITH AL-AHKAM (أَحَادِيثُ الأَحكَام)
LEGAL NARRATIONS

The aḥadīth that deal with law are termed aḥadīth al-aḥkām — narrations of a legal nature. These narrations explain, clarify, elaborate, and modify legal verses of the Quran. That is why early on in Islamic History a genre of ḥadīth literature came about known as sunan. A sunan is a ḥadīth collection that is organized according to the well-known chapters of fiqh or Islamic Jurisprudence. For example, ṭahārah (purification), ṣalah

49 33:21

50 al-Adab al-Mufrad, *b. man daʿā allāh an yuḥassin khulqah*, 308

51 68:4

(prayer), zakāh (obligatory charity), ṣawm (fasting), ḥajj (pilgrimage), nikāḥ (marriage), ṭalāq (divorce) and buyūʿ (transactions). The Book of ṭahārah will then have separate chapters for wuḍū' (ritual purification), tayammum (dry ritual purification), and ghusl (purificatory bath).

The Scholars of Uṣūl classify rulings found in aḥadīth into three categories:

1. THE SUNNAH CONSISTS OF RULINGS THAT CONFIRM AND REITERATE THOSE FOUND IN THE QURAN.

For example, all of the narrations regarding the five pillars (praying, fasting, zakāh and ḥajj), rights of one's parents, respect for the property of others, homicide, theft, and false testimony reaffirm the Quranic rules regarding these subjects.

A more specific example is the ḥadīth of the Prophet ﷺ,

وَلَا يَحِلُّ لِامْرِئٍ مِنْ مَالِ أَخِيهِ إِلَّا مَا طَابَتْ بِهِ نَفْسُهُ

"It is unlawful to take the property of a Muslim without their express consent"[52]

This ḥadīth affirms the verse of the Quran that tells us, "O you who have believed, do not consume one another's wealth unjustly but only [in lawful] business by mutual consent."[53] Similarly, the Prophet ﷺ said, "Act kindly towards women."[54] This ḥadīth affirms the Quranic injunction, "And live with them in kindness."

2. THE SUNNAH MAY CONSIST OF AN EXPLANATION OR CLARIFICATION OF THE QURAN

Some of the injunctions of the Quran may be what the scholars of Uṣūl classify as ambivalent (mujmal). The clarification or details of these rulings are often found in aḥadīth. For example, all of the aḥadīth that give specific details regarding acts of worship. Another example is that the Quran has laid

52 Aḥmad, *ḥadīth ʿamr bin yathribī*, 15488, al-Dārquṭnī, *k. al-buyūʿ*, 2885, 2886, and al-Bayhaqī, *k. al-ghaṣb, b. man ghaṣab layḥan f-adkhalah fī safīnah aw banā ʿalayh jidāran*, 11545

53 4:29

54 Muslim, 3468

down the general principle that sale is lawful and interest is unlawful. The Prophet ﷺ then explained the details regarding the rules of sale, including its conditions, varieties, and which might be considered ribā (interest).

The Sunnah of the Prophet ﷺ can also qualify or restrict some of the rules of the Quran that are mentioned in absolute or unrestricted terms. For example the Quran states, "[As for] the thief, the male and the female, amputate their hands in recompense for what they committed as a deterrent [punishment] from Allah. And Allah is Exalted in Might and Wise."[55] We learn through the companions that the Prophet ﷺ qualified this statement by specifying that the [right] hand should be cut from the wrist.[56] The Sunnah may also specify the general terms of the Quran.

3. THE SUNNAH MAY CONSIST OF RULINGS ON WHICH THE QURAN IS SILENT

For example, the prohibition of wearing gold and silk for men, Ṣadaqah al-Fiṭr, the right of preemption (shufʿah), and the grandmother's entitlement to a share in inheritance.

55 وَالسَّارِقُ وَالسَّارِقَةُ فَاقْطَعُوا أَيْدِيَهُمَا جَزَاءً بِمَا كَسَبَا نَكَالًا مِنَ اللَّهِ ۗ وَاللَّهُ عَزِيزٌ حَكِيمٌ 5:38

56 The recitation of Ibn Masʿūd ﵁ is "فاقطعوا أيمانهما," "cut their right hands." This is then further qualified, understood, and agreed upon by the Ṣaḥābah ﵃ based on the statements of Abū Bakr ﵁ and ʿUmar ﵁ that a thief's right hand should be amputated from the wrist. Ibn Qudāmah, *al-Mughnī* v. 9 p. 121

7

AL-IJMA:

CONSENSUS

The third source a jurist turns to when searching for and formulating a legal ruling is Ijmāʿ — consensus. When discussing Ijmāʿ, introductory books of Uṣūl highlight four aspects:

1. Definition
2. Conditions
3. Authority
4. Types

Linguistically, the word ijmāʿ comes from the Arabic verb "ajmaʿa", which has two different uses. It can be used to convey the meaning of "to determine" and "to resolve". For example, a person can say أجمع فلان على الأمر, "So and so decided on the matter." Similarly, in the Quran Allah ﷻ says, "So collectively agree to your plan."[57] In this context the word conveys the meaning to decide, determine, and resolve. It can also mean to agree upon something. For example, a person can say, "أجمع القوم على كذا" — the people agreed on such and such.

Technically, ijmāʿ is defined as,

57 فَأَجْمِعُوا أَمْرَكُم 10:71

اِتِّفَاقُ الْمُجتَهِدِينَ مِن أُمّةِ مُحَمَّدٍ ﷺ بَعدَ وَفَاتِهِ فِي عَصرٍ مِن
العُصُورِ عَلَى حُكمٍ شَرعِيٍ

The unanimous agreement of the mujtahids (independent jurists) of the Ummah of Muḥammad after his death in a specific era on a legal ruling.

When formulating definitions, the scholars were very specific in their choice of words. Every word or clause in the definition serves a specific purpose.

The first part of the definition "unanimous agreement" refers to the fact that there has to be a unanimous agreement on a specific matter. It can't be a partial agreement, or the agreement of a specific group of scholars, or even the scholars of a specific place or locality. It has to be every single mujtahid of that particular era. For example, it can't just be the consensus of the scholars of Madinah or the scholars of Iraq, or the consensus of the Rightly Guided Caliphs.[58]

The second part of the definition "of the Mujtahidūn" refers to the fact that the agreement has to come from the Mujtahidūn of a specific era who are qualified to do ijtihād.[59] Meaning, those legal jurists who have reached the level of having the ability to form independent rulings from their sources. That is why consideration is not given to the consensus of non-mujtahids, the general public, or even the members of a modern legal body.

The third part of the definition "of the Ummah of Muḥammad ﷺ" highlights that the mujtahidūn must be Muslim. This is quite obvious. The agreement of the jurists of another religion will not be considered ijmāʿ.

The fourth part of the definition "after the death of the Prophet ﷺ" highlights that a consensus that was reached during his life is not technically classified as ijmāʿ. If he ﷺ agreed with the Companions on an issue or affirmed their conclusion, then his agreement or affirmation was the source of the law, not the consensus. This agreement or affirmation is considered

58 That is to say that the ijmāʿ of a group of scholars from a certain city isn't a binding proof for all Muslims at all times. One can say that all of the scholars of Kūfah agreed on a certain ruling, and that holds some legal weight to those scholars to a certain degree.

59 This is crucial and needs to be understood properly because it is not the consensus of every scholar. Scholars who are experts in the field of only Qur'ānic sciences, or only Ḥadīth, or only History are not considered a part of this unanimity. In the same way that scholars of Fiqh and Law are not considered in the consensus of matters that deal with the recitation of the Qur'ān.

to be part of the Sunnah. During his lifetime, the Prophet ﷺ alone was the highest authority regarding the Sharīʿah.

The fifth part of the definition "on a legal ruling" refers to the fact that the consensus should be regarding a legal matter. This excludes the consensus upon a linguistic or medical matter.

CONDITIONS FOR THE VALIDITY OF IJMA

From this definition, the scholars of Uṣūl argue that in order for Ijmāʿ to be valid it has to meet the following six conditions:

1. Those undertaking Ijmāʿ must be a group of mujtahids. There has to be an actual group or body of mujtahids involved. It can't just be one or two people because having consensus is impossible with just one person.
2. The consensus has to be reached by all of the mujtahids upon the legal ruling. It has to be unanimous consensus. It can't be just the majority.
3. The consensus has to be unanimous amongst the mujtahids during the time of the actual issue itself.
4. All the mujtahids have to express their opinions regarding the matter explicitly or implicitly. This may be verbal, in writing, or in actuality (when a judge gives a ruling).
5. The mujtahids who have reached a consensus must be upright.[60]
6. The consensus has to be based upon some sort of legal precedent from the Quran and Sunnah.

Now, after looking at these conditions, naturally the question comes to mind, with such strict conditions how is it possible for Ijmāʿ to ever take place? This question will be addressed later on. However, classically, this is how the jurists envisioned and formulated the concept of Ijmāʿ.

60 Again, this is to ensure that no one-off scholar with heretical views nullifies ijmāʿ. Similarly a scholar who has lost their sanity, has become senile, or is in the pangs of death are not included.

MUSTANAD AL-IJMA (مُستَنَدُ الإجماع): **THE BASIS OF IJMA**

As mentioned above, one of the conditions for Ijmāʿ to be valid is that it has to be based on some sort of legal precedent. The Ijmāʿ has to be built on a solid foundation; it has to be rooted in the Quran and Sunnah with some sort of textual authority. This foundation or textual authority is referred to as mustanad al-Ijmāʿ. It is the proof, source, or root the mujtahids use in order to arrive at their consensus.

Generally speaking, it would be very improbable for there to be a consensus upon an issue without some sort of cause that would lead to an agreement; something that would unite people's opinions or views. The mustanad is that cause. It can be a verse from the Quran or a ḥadīth of the Prophet ﷺ. If it is coming from a definitive proof then the Ijmāʿ would serve to reaffirm and add strength to the legal ruling. If it is coming from a speculative proof it can add strength to it making it into something that would be considered definitive. It enhances their authority and makes them binding.

TYPES OF IJMA

Ijmāʿ is divided into two types on the basis of the way it was formed or on the basis of the way consensus was reached:

1. Explicit Ijmāʿ (al-Ijmāʿ al-Ṣarīḥ)
2. Tacit Ijmāʿ (al-Ijmāʿ al-Sukūtī)

1. EXPLICIT IJMĀʿ (الإجماعُ الصَّرِيحُ)

This occurs when the mujtahids agree on the ruling of a specific issue explicitly through their statements. For example, if all the mujtahids came together to discuss a certain legal issue and they all explicitly agreed upon the ruling. Every single member of the gathering expressed their opinion verbally. It can also happen if a certain legal issue came up in a certain time period, and all the mujtahids of that time issued a similar fatwa regarding it. This type of Ijmāʿ is considered to be a source of law that is necessary to follow.

2. *TACIT IJMĀʿ* (الإِجمَاعُ السُّكُوتِيّ)

This form of Ijmāʿ takes place when some mujtahids, one or more, issue a verdict on a legal ruling and the rest of the mujtahids come to know of it, but they choose to remain silent; they neither affirm it nor refute it. In this scenario their silence is considered to be tacit approval.

AUTHORITY OF IJMA

According to the vast majority of scholars, if Ijmāʿ takes place the way it has been described, fulfilling these conditions, it becomes a binding legal proof. It is considered obligatory to act upon the Ijmāʿ and its opposition is prohibited. Also, an issue that has been agreed upon through Ijmāʿ can't be undone and subject to ijtihād once again. The scholars of Uṣūl write, "Ijmāʿ ensures the correct interpretation of the Quran, the faithful understanding and transmission of the Sunnah, and the legitimate use of ijtihād."

There are a number of proofs from the Quran and Sunnah that establish the authority of Ijmāʿ as a legal proof. In one verse, Allah ﷻ says :

يَا أَيُّهَا الَّذِينَ آمَنُوا أَطِيعُوا اللَّهَ وَأَطِيعُوا الرَّسُولَ وَأُولِي الْأَمْرِ مِنكُمْ ۖ فَإِن تَنَازَعْتُمْ فِي شَيْءٍ فَرُدُّوهُ إِلَى اللَّهِ وَالرَّسُولِ إِن كُنتُمْ تُؤْمِنُونَ بِاللَّهِ وَالْيَوْمِ الْآخِرِ ۚ ذَٰلِكَ خَيْرٌ وَأَحْسَنُ تَأْوِيلًا

O you who believe, obey Allah and obey the Messenger and those in authority among you. And if you disagree over anything, refer it back to Allah and the Messenger, if you believe in Allah and the Last Day. That is the best way and best result.[61]

Just as Allah ﷻ has commanded believers to obey Allah and His Messenger ﷺ, He has also commanded them to obey "those in authority amongst you." And those in authority amongst them, in terms of fatwa and ijtihād, are the scholars who are qualified to do so. In another verse, Allah ﷻ says:

61 4:59

وَمَن يُشَاقِقِ الرَّسُولَ مِن بَعْدِ مَا تَبَيَّنَ لَهُ الْهُدَىٰ وَيَتَّبِعْ غَيْرَ سَبِيلِ
الْمُؤْمِنِينَ نُوَلِّهِ مَا تَوَلَّىٰ وَنُصْلِهِ جَهَنَّمَ ۖ وَسَاءَتْ مَصِيرًا

And whoever opposes the Messenger after guidance has become clear to him and follows other than the way of the believers - We will give him what he has taken and drive him into Hell, and evil it is as a destination.[62]

In this verse Allah ﷻ has made following a path or a way other than the way of the Muslims equivalent to opposing Allah and His Messenger. The commentators mention that the "way of the believers" refers to their agreement and the way that they have chosen; in other words, their consensus.

The reasoning goes that if opposing Allah and His messenger is a sin, then following a path other than the path of the Muslims is also a sin. Therefore it is necessary to follow the path of the Muslims collectively, which is considered to be Ijmāʿ. Imām al-Shāfiʿī argued that this verse provides clear authority for Ijmāʿ.

There are also a number of authentic narrations that mention that the Ummah of Muḥammad ﷺ will not unanimously agree on a mistake. There are so many narrations regarding this concept that the scholars say it has reached the level of tawātur, but by meaning. Take the following narrations for example:

من فارقَ الجماعةَ شبرًا فمات إلا مات ميتةً جاهليةٍ مَنْ فَارَقَ
الْجَمَاعَةَ شِبْرًا فَمَاتَ إِلاَّ مَاتَ مِيتَةً جَاهِلِيَّةً

Whoever disbands from the community by a mere handspan and dies, has died a death of ignorance.[63]

لا يَزَالُ مِنْ أُمَّتِي أُمَّةٌ قَايِمَةٌ بِأَمْرِ اللَّهِ مَا يَضُرُّهُمْ مَنْ كَذَّبَهُمْ وَلاَ
مَنْ خَالَفَهُمْ حَتَّى يَأْتِيَ أَمْرُ اللَّهِ وَهُمْ عَلَى ذَلِكَ

62 4:115

63 Bukhārī, *k. al-fitan, b. qawl al-nabiyy* ﷺ *satarawna baʿdī umūran tunkirūnaha*, 7054

A group of my Ummah will continue standing firm to the commands of God. They will not be phased by those who deny them, reject them, or disagree with them until God sends His Decree while they remain like that, standing firm.[64]

إِنَّ اللَّهَ لاَ يَجْمَعُ أُمَّتِي - أَوْ قَالَ أُمَّةَ مُحَمَّدٍ - عَلَى ضَلاَلَةٍ وَيَدُ اللَّهِ مَعَ الْجَمَاعَةِ وَمَنْ شَذَّ شَذَّ إِلَى النَّارِ

Indeed Allah will not let my community gather upon an error and the hand of Allah is with the community. However breakaway isolated, has gone alone to the Fire.[65]

فَإِنَّ الشَّيْطَانَ مَعَ الْوَاحِدِ وَهُوَ مِنَ الاِثْنَيْنِ أَبْعَدُ مَنْ أَرَادَ بُحْبُوحَةَ الْجَنَّةِ فَلْيَلْزَمِ الْجَمَاعَةَ

Indeed Satan sticks to the lone individual, but is further away from two. Whoever dreams of having the best spot in Jannah should stick to the community.[66]

إِنَّ أُمَّتِي لَنْ تَجْتَمِعَ عَلَى ضَلاَلَةٍ فَإِذَا رَأَيْتُمُ اخْتِلاَفًا فَعَلَيْكُمْ بِالسَّوَادِ الأَعْظَمِ

My community will never agree upon an error/mistake. If you're faced with a disputed matter, stick with the undeniable majority of Muslims.[67]

قَالَ بنُ مَسعُودٍ رَضِىَ اللهُ عَنهُ: مَا رَآهُ المُسلِمُونَ حَسَنًا فَهُوَ عِندَ اللهِ حَسَنٌ

64 Bukhārī, *k. al-tawḥīd b. qawl Allāh taʿālā: innmā qawluna li-shayʾ idhā aradnāh kun fa-yakūn*, 7460

65 Tirmidhī, *k. al-fitan ʿan Rasūlillah, b. mā jā'a fī luzūm al-jamāʿah*, 2167

66 Tirmidhī, *k. al-fitan, b. mā jā'a fī luzūm al-jamāʿah*, 2165

67 Ibn Mājah, *k. al-fitan b. al-sawād al-aʿẓam*, 3950

Whatever the Muslims deem to be good is good in the sight of Allah.[68]

Based on these verses and narrations, as well as other narrations, Ijmāʿ is established as a source of law.

POSSIBILITY OF IJMA OCCURRING

Based off what has been covered, it seems that the possibility of Ijmāʿ occurring is highly improbable. This objection arises because of some of the stringent conditions stipulated for the validity of Ijmāʿ. For example, one of the conditions is that in order for Ijmāʿ to be valid it has to be the consensus of all the mujtahids of a specific time period. This creates difficulties: how is a mujtahid identified and who decides who is a mujtahid and who is not? Similarly, it is very difficult to ascertain the opinion of every single mujtahid on a specific legal matter. That is why some argue that it is impossible for Ijmāʿ to take place.

The main response to these objections is that they hold no weight against something that has actually occurred in history. The Companions ﷺ reached Ijmāʿ on a number of different issues:

1. Fighting those who refused to pay zakāh during the time of Abū Bakr ﷺ
2. Compiling the Quran into a single volume
3. The impermissibility of interest in six specific types of commodities
4. The impermissibility of a Muslim woman marrying a non-Muslim man
5. The validity of a marriage without mentioning the amount of mahr
6. The impermissibility of combining a woman with her paternal aunt and maternal aunt in a marriage
7. The impermissibility of using pig fat
8. The grandmother receiving 1/6th in inheritance
9. The impermissibility of selling food before taking possession

Some scholars are of the opinion that Ijmāʿ according to this particular definition really only took place amongst the Companions ﷺ. To claim Ijmāʿ in an era or time period after theirs would be difficult to prove and even

---

68 al-Haythamī, Majmaʿ al-Zawāʾid, 182

more difficult to actually take place. That is why it is extremely difficult to prove Ijmāʿ on specific issues that are open to ijtihād.

Historically, Ijmāʿ has often been claimed for rulings on which only a majority, not universal, consensus had existed within or beyond a particular school. Some modern day scholars also make the case for Ijmāʿ to take place today through conferences and seminars that invite qualified and trained scholars from every part of the Muslim world to discuss issues and determine their legal rulings.

8

AL-QIYAS: ANALOGICAL DEDUCTION

As mentioned earlier, when a jurist is searching for a legal ruling regarding a specific issue they first turn to the Quran. If they can't find it in the Quran they turn to the Sunnah, then Ijmāʿ, and finally Qiyās. When discussing the concept of Qiyās the scholars of Uṣūl talk about its definition, elements, and authority.

DEFINITION

Linguistically the word Qiyās come from the Arabic verb "qāsa, yaqīsu", which literally means "to measure" or "ascertain the length, weight or quality of something". Measuring something against some sort of scale. For example, قِستُ الثَّوبَ بِالمِترِ "I measured the cloth with the meter." It can also mean to compare two things that are equal or similar. For example, it can be said زَيدٌ يَقِيسُ عَلَى خَالِدٍ فِي عَقلِهِ وَعَمَلِهِ "Zaid and Khālid are comparable in intelligence and knowledge." Linguistically the word itself suggests an equality or similarity between two things where one is used to evaluate the other.

Technically, Qiyās is defined as the extension of a legal ruling from an existing case (al-aṣl) to a new case (al-farʿ) on the basis of a common effective cause (ʿillah).

هو تعدية الحكم من الأصل إلى الفرع لعلة متحدة

If the texts of the Quran, Sunnah, or Ijmāʿ contain a case whose effective cause is known to a mujtahid, then he/she comes across a new case that shares the same effective cause, they can assign the legal ruling of the original case to the new case. The original case is regulated by a text and Qiyās extends the same legal ruling to the new case because of the common effective cause. From this it is understood that Qiyās is only used when the legal ruling of a new case is not found in the Quran, Sunnah, or Ijmāʿ. Qiyās is simply the extension of an existing law.

ELEMENTS OF QIYAS

Based on this definition Qiyās involves four elements:

1. al-Aṣl (الأَصلُ): The original case whose ruling is mentioned in a text from the Quran, Sunnah, or Ijmāʿ. It is also referred to as the maqīs ʿalayh or the case upon which the analogy has been built.
2. al-ʿIllah (العِلَّةُ): The effective cause, which is the underlying cause that leads to the ruling. This is the most significant player in the whole process of Qiyās. It is literally the direct cause of the legal ruling.

When discussing the ʿillah, it is extremely important to recognize the difference between the effective cause of a ruling and its potential wisdoms. When looking at a particular legal ruling it can have certain objectives or wisdoms behind it. Sometimes these objectives and wisdoms may be known and sometimes they may be unknown. Sometimes they may be present and sometimes they might not. For example, there is a particular right known as the right of shufʿah — preemption. The joint or neighboring owner of a property has first priority in purchasing the property whenever the partner or neighbor wishes to sell it. The effective cause is being a joint owner or the neighbor. The ḥikmah, or wisdom, behind this ruling is to protect the partner or neighbor against any possible harm that can arise from sale to a third party. Now this harm could materialize or it may not. Regardless of whether this harm exists or not, the partner or neighbor will still be entitled to the right of shufʿah.

Based on this distinction between the ʿillah and the ḥikmah, the scholars of Uṣūl developed the following principle:

الأَحكَامُ تَدُورُ عَلَى العِلَلِ لا عَلَى الحِكَمِ

Legal rulings are based on their effective causes not on their objectives (wisdoms).

One of the reasons for this is that the ʿillah is something that is always constant. The ḥikmah, on the other hand, is not constant nor is it necessarily specified. That is why if the ʿillah is found, the ḥukm (legal ruling) will also be there even though the ḥikmah (wisdom) may not be. For example, if a person is travelling, as a concession they do not have to fast. The ḥikmah behind the ruling is to protect the traveller from unnecessary hardship. But hardship is something that is very subjective. That is why the concession is attached to the travel itself, which is the ʿillah and not the wisdom, the hardship.

Perhaps a practical example might make the concept a little more clear. The ʿillah or the effective cause for stopping at a traffic light is the red light itself. The ḥikmah is to prevent accidents. If a person breaks a red light they are committing a crime regardless of whether or not there was actually an accident.

3. al-Farʿ (الفَرعُ): The new case whose ruling is not mentioned in a text from the Quran, Sunnah, or Ijmāʿ. This is also called the maqīs, the case for which the analogy is constructed. It must be something whose ruling has not been explicitly mentioned.
4. al-Ḥukm (الحُكمُ): The ruling mentioned in the text for the original case that is extended to the new case.

Example 1:

The Quran explicitly prohibits drinking wine (الخمر). Allah ﷻ says, "Believers! Intoxicants, gambling, [sacrificing on] stone altars [to other than Allah], and divining arrows are defilement from Satan! Shun and refrain from them so you can be successful."[69] The ʿillah, effective cause, for the prohibition of wine is the fact that it is an intoxicant (muskir). The reason why it is prohibited is because it is an intoxicant. This prohibition is then extended to narcotics because they are also intoxicants. Thus, narcotics are also prohibited.

In this example the original case (aṣl) is drinking wine. The effective cause (ʿillah) is the intoxicating effect. The new case (farʿ) is taking narcotics. The ruling (ḥukm) is prohibition. So the prohibition of drinking wine is extended by analogy (Qiyās) to drugs because of the shared effective cause, which is the intoxicating effect.

Example 2:

The Prophet ﷺ said, "The murderer will not inherit (from his victim)."[70]

الْقَاتِلُ لاَ يَرِثُ

This ḥadīth explicitly prohibits the heir from receiving inheritance from his victim who he would normally inherit from. The murdering heir will be deprived from his inheritance. This ruling is extended by Qiyās to bequests, which means that the murderer can't benefit from the victim's will as well because of the shared effective cause, which is hastening death through a criminal act (murder).

In this example the aṣl is the case mentioned in the ḥadīth; murdering the one who he will inherit from. The ʿillah or the effective cause is the act of murder. The farʿ is murdering the one who has made a bequest in their will. The ḥukm is deprivation of benefit.

Example 3:

It is prohibited to propose to a woman who has already been proposed to by another man. The Prophet ﷺ said, "A man should not [knowingly] propose to a woman who has already been proposed to by his Muslim brother.

---

69 5:90 يَا أَيُّهَا الَّذِينَ آمَنُوا إِنَّمَا الْخَمْرُ وَالْمَيْسِرُ وَالْأَنصَابُ وَالْأَزْلَامُ رِجْسٌ مِّنْ عَمَلِ الشَّيْطَانِ فَاجْتَنِبُوهُ لَعَلَّكُمْ تُفْلِحُون

70 Tirmidhī, *k. al-farā'iḍ ʿan rasūlillah*, 2109

That is, until he marries her, does not pursue, or allows him to."[71]

وَلاَ يَخْطُبَ الرَّجُلُ عَلَى خِطْبَةِ أَخِيهِ حَتَّى يَتْرُكَ الخَاطِبُ قَبْلَهُ أَوْ
يَأْذَنَ لَهُ الخَاطِبُ

The effective cause of this legal ruling is to prevent harm to a person's interests and to prevent conflict and hostility between individuals. Through Qiyās the same ruling can be extended to any transaction in which the same effective cause is found.

Example 4:

The Quran prohibits buying or selling goods after the call to Friday Prayer. God said, "rush towards the mention of God, and abstain from (bayʿ) trade".[72] The effective cause is taking people away from the prayer. This ruling can be extended to anything else that would take a person away from the Friday Prayer.

AUTHORITY OF QIYAS

Where does Qiyās get its authority from? Why is it considered to be one of the primary sources of Islamic Law? The authority of Qiyās is found in the Quran, Sunnah, Ijmāʿ, and rational reasoning.

The following verses of the Quran are used to prove the authority of Qiyās:

1. "O you who have believed, obey Allah and obey the Messenger and those in authority among you. If you disagree over something, refer it back to Allah and the Messenger, if you truly believe in Allah and the Last Day. That is the best [way] and best in result."[73]

   The portion of the verse used for proving the authority of Qiyās is "And if you disagree over anything, refer it to Allah and the Messenger." The only way to refer a disagreement to Allah and His messenger is by using base cases, and foundational rulings found

71 Bukhārī, *k. al-nikāḥ, b. lā yakhṭub ʿalā khiṭbah akhīhī*, 5142-5144

72 62:9

73 4:59

in the Quran and Sunnah. One way of doing so is to identify the underlying reason behind a legal ruling and apply it to the disagreed upon matter.

2. "Indeed, We have revealed to you, [O Muhammad], the Book with the truth so you judge between people by that which Allah has shown you. And do not advocate for those who are deceitful."[74]

   Qiyās is a way to "judge between people by that which Allah has shown." A judgment can be based on guidance that Allah ﷻ has clearly given or on that which resembles it very closely.

3. "So take lesson (consider), O people of vision!"[75] "Consideration" is this context means attention to similarities and comparison between similar things.

4. In several places the Quran mentions the rationale behind rulings explicitly or by referring to its objectives. The jurists conclude that mentioning the rationale behind rulings and referring to its objectives would be meaningless if they weren't observed and followed as a guide for determining the rulings of issues that aren't mentioned in the Quran and Sunnah.

Scholars from the four schools of thought use these verses and others similar to them to prove the authority of Qiyās.

From the Sunnah, scholars use the following narrations as proof for the authority of Qiyās:

1. Muʿādh ibn Jabal رضي الله عنه narrated that when the Prophet ﷺ sent him to Yemen he asked, "How will you judge when the occasion of deciding a case arises?" He replied, "I shall judge in accordance with Allah's Book." He asked, "(What will you do) if you do not find any guidance in Allah's Book?" He replied, "(I shall act) in accordance with the Sunnah of the Messenger of Allah ﷺ." He asked, "(What will you do) if you do not find any guidance in the Sunnah of the Messenger of Allah ﷺ and in Allah's Book?" He replied, "I shall do my best to form an opinion and I shall spare no effort." The Messenger of Allah ﷺ then patted him on the breast and said, "Praise be to Allah

---

74 إِنَّا أَنزَلْنا إِلَيكَ الْكِتَابَ بِالْحَقِّ لِتَحْكُمَ بَيْنَ النَّاسِ بِمَا أَرَاكَ اللَّهُ ۚ وَلَا تَكُن لِّلْخَائِنِينَ خَصِيمًا 4:105

75 فَاعْتَبِرُوا يَا أُولِي الْأَبْصَار 59:2

Who has helped the messenger of the Messenger of Allah to find something which pleases the Messenger of Allah."[76]

2. Once a man from Khath''am came to the Prophet ﷺ and said that his father had accepted Islam and because of his old age he is unable to perform ḥajj. So he asked, "Should I perform ḥajj on his behalf?" The Prophet ﷺ asked, "Are you his eldest child?" He said, "Yes." The Prophet ﷺ said, "Suppose if your father had a debt and you paid it on his behalf. Would that benefit him?" He said, "Yes." He ﷺ responded, "The debt owed to Allah is more deserving of being paid."[77]
3. Once ʿUmar ؓ asked if kissing invalidates the fast. The Prophet ﷺ asked, "What if you gargle water while fasting?" ʿUmar ؓ responded, "There's no harm in that." The Prophet ﷺ said, "The answer to your first question is the same."[78]

The authority of Qiyās is also established through Ijmāʿ. According to the scholars of Uṣūl, the Companions ؓ reached a consensus on the validity of Qiyās as is seen through several instances. For example, Abū Bakr ؓ drew an analogy between the father and grandfather in respect to their entitlement of inheritance. ʿUmar ؓ wrote a very well-known letter to Abū Musa al-Ashʿarī when he appointed him as the governor of Basra. In it he wrote, اعرف الأشباه والنظائر وقس الأمور برأيك "Determine the similitudes for purposes of analogy." Similarly, the Companions ؓ held a council to set a fixed punishment for drinking wine. ʿAlī ؓ suggested that the penalty of false accusation should be applied to one who drinks wine through analogy. "When a person gets drunk, he raves, and when he raves he accuses falsely."

The scholars of Uṣūl also offered several rational arguments for the authority and validity of Qiyās. For example, they argue that the vast majority of legal rulings in the Sharīʿah can be understood rationally. If the rationale of a legal ruling is understood, that same ruling should apply anywhere else that same rationale is found.

They also argue that Qiyās is what allows for the Sharīʿah to be applicable for all times and places. It is a tool that is used that creates flexibility within the Sharīʿah.

---

76 Abū Dāwūd, *k. al-aqḍiyah, b. ijtihād al-ra'y fī al-qaḍā'a*, 3592

77 al-Bayhaqi, *al-Sunan al-Kubra*, 4/329

78 Abū Dāwūd, *k. al-sawm, b. al-qublah li al-sa'im*, 2385

The Quran, Sunnah, Ijmāʿ, and Qiyās are the four primary agreed upon sources of law. The next few chapters will discuss those sources of law that are not unanimously agreed upon starting with Istiḥsān.

9

AL-ISTIHSAN: JURISTIC PREFERENCE

Linguistically, the word istiḥsān is derived from the verb "istaḥsana/yastaḥsinu", which means to consider something to be nice, good, or appropriate. The word istiḥsān itself means to consider something good.

Technically, the scholars of Uṣūl have defined it in a few different ways:

1. Leaving the ruling of a particular Qiyās for a Qiyās that is stronger than it, or specifying Qiyās because of a proof stronger than it.
2. Leaving Qiyās because of a stronger proof from the Quran, Sunnah, or Ijmāʿ.
3. A principle that authorizes departure from an established precedent in favor of a different ruling for a reason stronger than the one which is obtained in the precedent.

The third definition seems to be the most comprehensive. The precedent which is set aside by Istiḥsān is based on an analogy that can be left while giving preference to a stronger proof such as the Quran, Sunnah, necessity, or a stronger Qiyās. This could happen by giving preference to an obscure analogy over a clear analogy, or by making an exception to a general rule. Qiyās Jaliy (Clear Analogy) is a straightforward analogy that is very easily understood. Qiyās Khafiy (Obscure Analogy) is a more subtle form of analogy in the sense that it is not obvious but becomes clear through deeper reflection. Based off this, Istiḥsān is a departure from a Qiyās Jaliy to a Qiyās Khafiy. When a jurist is faced with a new issue they search for a precedent and try to find the legal ruling through Qiyās. Their search may lead to two different outcomes based on these different types of analogies. This is one form of Istiḥsān.

The other type of Istiḥsān is to make an exception to a general rule or principle because of a text, ijmāʿ, custom, necessity, or public interest. An easier way to explain it is making an exception to a general rule of existing law. It is a form of ijtihād that gives preference to the best of various solutions that may exist for a particular problem.

Examples:

1. According to the general rule in order for a contract of sale to be valid the item must actually exist. However, an exception is made for the contract of istiṣnāʿ, the contract for manufacturing goods. The contract for manufacturing goods is described as when someone places an order for a certain commodity to be made at a price determined at the time of the contract.
2. According to the Ḥanafīs, the endowment (waqf) of cultivated land includes the transfer of all the ancillary rights (easements) that are attached to the property. For example, the right of water, the right of passage, and the right of flow are all included although they aren't explicitly mentioned in the contract. This particular ruling is based off istiḥsān, or Qiyās Khafi. According to the rules of sale, the object of the contract has to be clearly identified in detail. What is not explicitly specified in the contract is not automatically included. There is a direct analogy between a waqf and a sale because both involve the transfer of ownership. According to this analogy the attached rights can only be included in the waqf if they are explicitly identified.

   However, this analogy would lead to a number of difficulties. The waqf of cultivated land without the attached rights would prevent the basic purpose of the waqf, which is to facilitate the use of the property for charitable purposes. To avoid these difficulties the jurists use an alternative analogy, Qiyās Khafi. They base the analogy on the contract of lease (ijārah) not the contract of sale, because both involve the transfer of usufruct (intifāʿ).

AUTHORITY

There is no direct or explicit authority for Istiḥsān in the Quran or in the Sunnah, but jurists have quoted both in favor it.

Scholars use the following verses as a basis for the validity and authority of Istiḥsān:

1. "Allah intends ease for you and does not intend hardship."[80] The argument presented is that utilizing istiḥsān is a way of facilitating ease and avoiding difficulty.
2. "Those who listen to Quran and Ḥadīth (al-qawl) and follow it perfectly. Those are the ones Allah has guided, those are people of understanding."[81]
3. "And follow the best of what has been revealed to you from your Lord."[82]

80 يُرِيدُ اللَّهُ بِكُمُ الْيُسْرَ وَلَا يُرِيدُ بِكُمُ الْعُسْرَ 2:185
81 الَّذِينَ يَسْتَمِعُونَ الْقَوْلَ فَيَتَّبِعُونَ أَحْسَنَهُ ۚ أُولَٰئِكَ الَّذِينَ هَدَاهُمُ اللَّهُ ۖ وَأُولَٰئِكَ هُمْ أُولُو الْأَلْبَابِ 39:18
82 وَاتَّبِعُوا أَحْسَنَ مَا أُنزِلَ إِلَيْكُم مِّن رَّبِّكُم 39:15

10

AL-MASLAHAH AL-MURSALAH:

PUBLIC INTEREST

Linguistically, the word "maṣlaḥah" means benefit or interest. The word "mursalah" means absolute. As a compound structure al-maṣlaḥah al-mursalah means absolute benefit or absolute best interest.

الوصف الذى يلائم تصرفات الشرع و مقاصده و لكن لم يشهد له
دليل معين من الشرع و يحصل من ربط الحكم به جلب مصلحة أو
دفع مفسدة عن الناس

Technically, it is defined as a consideration that is proper and harmonious with the objectives of the Sharīʿah; however, there is no specific evidence for it from the Sharīʿah, yet the ruling associated with it secures a benefit or prevents a harm. Imām al-Ghazālī ﷺ mentions that it consists of considerations that secure a benefit or prevent a harm but which are simultaneously harmonious with the objectives of the Sharīʿah. These objectives are the protection of religion, life, intellect, lineage, and property.

For example, the Companions ﷺ agreed unanimously to compile the Quran, issue currency, keep court registers, and establish prisons because of overwhelming public interest.[83] al-Maṣlaḥah al-Mursalah is also known as

83 These instances are well known through the biographies of the Companions ﷺ and books of history.

Istiṣlāḥ.

It is extremely important to note that maṣlaḥah is not considered a proof when it comes to devotional matters (acts of worship), and specific injunctions of the Sharīʿah. That is why the texts that mention issues such as prescribed penalties, expiation, fixed entitlements in inheritance, and the waiting period lie outside the scope of istiṣlāḥ.

TYPES OF MASLAHAH

If certain interests (maṣāliḥ) form the basis of legal rulings found in the Quran and Sunnah and there is proof that these interests were considered and upheld as reasons behind the law, then they are called recognized interests (المصالح المعتبرة).

The maṣāliḥ are generally divided into three categories:

1. AL-ḌARŪRĪYĀT (الضروريات): ABSOLUTE ESSENTIALS

The Absolute Essentials are those interests or benefits upon which the lives of individuals depend, and whose neglect would lead to disorder and chaos in their lives. These include the five primary objectives of the Sharīʿah, which are the protection of:

1. religion
2. life
3. intellect
4. lineage
5. property

2. AL-ḤĀJIYĀT (الحاجيات): THE COMPLEMENTARY

These are interests or benefits that people need in order to remove hardships from them. It refers to those interests whose neglect leads to some type of hardship in life and not to ruin and disorder. For example, the concessions that are granted in some acts of worship such as shortening prayer for travellers, the option not to fast for a traveller, or even wiping over leather socks. All of these are concessions aimed at preventing hardship.

3. *AL-TAḤSĪNĀT* (التحسينات)*: EMBELLISHMENTS*

These are interests or benefits whose realization leads to improvement and attainment of those things that are desirable. For example, the observance of cleanliness in personal appearance and acts of worship, moral virtues, good character, and moderation.

The Sharīʿah, in its entirety, aims to uphold these interests and prevent harm. The jurists unanimously agree that promoting and protecting these interests can serve as a basis of forming legislation.

AUTHORITY OF ISTISLAH

Istiṣlāḥ derives its authority from the fact that the basic objective of legislation in Islam is to secure the welfare of people by securing their interests or by removing harm. The purpose behind the Sharīʿah is to promote welfare and prevent corruption. This is essentially the message of the verse that describes the prophethood of Muhammad ﷺ. The following verses are provided as evidence for the authority of Istiṣlāḥ:

1. "And We have not sent you, [O Muhammad], except as a grace to all of creation."[84]
2. "[God] has not placed extreme difficulty upon you in regards to religion."[85]
3. "Allah does not intend difficulty for you."[86]
4. "Allah intends ease for you, and does not intend hardship for you."[87]

84 21:107
85 22:78
86 2:185
87 65:7

11

'URF: SOCIETAL CUSTOM & NORMS

Linguistically, the word "'urf" means that which is known, familiar, or common. The jurists define 'urf as recurring practices that are acceptable to people of sound nature. It is the collective practice of a large number of people.

'Urf is only considered to be a valid source of law when it does not go against the principles of the Sharīʿah. It can serve as the basis of a legal ruling, but in a limited sense. Customs that don't go against the teachings of the Quran and Sunnah are acceptable as a basis of law.

For example, 'urf is used to determine the amount of expenditure that a husband must provide for his wife. Allah ﷻ says in the Quran, "Wealthy men should give and spend (on their wives) based on their wealth. Those who have limited resources should spend based on what Allah has provided for them."[88] This verse doesn't specify the exact amount of maintenance, so the scholars deem it to be determined by custom; that which women of a similar social and family status received.

The rules of fiqh that are based in juristic opinion, speculative analogy, and ijtihād are often formulated in the light of prevailing custom. The most important thing to keep in mind is that custom cannot violate a definitive text. For example, a person cannot say that drinking alcohol or dealing with

88 65:7

interest is permissible because they are the common practices in society.

TYPES OF 'URF

Initially ʿurf is divided into two types:

Verbal Custom (العرف القولى)
Actual Custom (العرف الفعلى)

1. VERBAL CUSTOM (العرف القولى)

Refers to the general agreement of people on the usage and meaning of words that aren't used in their literal sense. The customary meaning becomes dominant and the original or literal meaning becomes an exception. Whenever words that have acquired a different meaning in customary usage occur in contracts, oaths and commercial transactions their customary meanings will take preference.

For example, if someone says, "I swear I will never set foot in Muhammad's house!" According to custom this means they won't enter Muhammad's house. If they literally just place their foot inside of Muhammad's house they will not have broken their oath.

2. ACTUAL CUSTOM (العرف الفعلى)

Refers to commonly recurrent practices that are accepted by the people. For example, a give and take sale that is known as بيع التعاطى. This is a sale that takes place without verbalizing the offer and the acceptance.

Custom definitely plays a role in the formation of law but its role is not unrestricted. It is restricted and limited to certain situations and circumstances.

12

SHAR‘ MAN QABLANA:

REVEALED LAW OF THOSE BEFORE US

Sharʿ man Qablana refers to the legal rulings legislated by Allah ﷻ for previous nations through revelation to their Prophets such as Mūsa ﷺ and ʿĪsa ﷺ. It is the body of laws that were sent to previous prophets and nations through revelation.

There is a slight difference of opinion among jurists about the relationship of these previously revealed laws with the Sharīʿah. Are they considered to be a part of the Sharīʿah or has the Sharīʿah abrogated them? The reason why this discussion arises is because, in principle, all divinely revealed laws come from the same source, Allah ﷻ. Each system of law that has been revealed shares a common basic message; to affirm the oneness of Allah, believe in prophethood, believe in the last day, and the need for divine guidance to regulate human conduct.

The common nature of each divinely revealed religion is expressed in several places throughout the Quran. Allah says, "In matters of faith, He has laid down for you [people] the same commandment that He gave Noah, which We have revealed to you [Muhammad] and which We enjoined on Abraham and Moses and Jesus: 'Uphold the faith and do not be divided'."[89] Similarly, Allah ﷻ says, "Those were the people Allah guided, so follow the guidance they received."[90]

89 42:13
90 6:90

Although they shared common themes each system of law had its differences in terms of what was permissible and impermissible, and acts of worship. The jurists divide Sharʿ man Qablana into two categories:

1. Those rulings that aren't mentioned in the Quran and Sunnah: There is unanimous agreement that these rulings aren't applicable to Muslims. The laws of previous revelations are not applicable to Muslims unless they are specifically upheld by the Sharīʿah.
2. Those rulings that are mentioned in the Quran and Sunnah - The Quran and Sunnah make reference to rulings of previous nations in three different ways.
    a. The Quran and Sunnah may refer to a ruling of previous nations and simultaneously make it obligatory on us as well. These laws are binding upon Muslims just as they were binding upon previous nations. Meaning, the Sharīʿah affirmed them.

       For example, Allah ﷻ says, "O you who have believed, decreed upon you is fasting as it was decreed upon those before you that you may become righteous."[91] An example from the Sunnah is the ḥadīth that makes sacrifice by slaughtering animals lawful for us as well. The Companions of the Messenger of Allah ﷺ said, "O Messenger of Allah, what are these sacrifices?" He said, "The Sunnah of your father Ibrahim." They said, "What is there for us in them, O Messenger of Allah?" He said, "For every hair, one merit." They said, "What about wool, O Messenger of Allah?" He said, "For every hair of wool, one merit."[92]
    b. Those rules that have been mentioned but have been abrogated in our Sharīʿah. These rules are not applicable to Muslims. For example, the Quran mentions certain varieties of food that were prohibited for the Jews but not for Muslims. Similarly, taking the spoils of war was prohibited for previous nations and has been made permissible for Muslims. The Prophet ﷺ said, "The spoils of war have been

91 2:183

92 ibn Majah, *k. al-adahi*, 3247

made permissible for me and they weren't permissible for anyone before me."[93]

أحلت لى الغنائم و لم تحل لأحد من قبلى

c. The Quran and Sunnah mention rulings from previous nations without upholding them or abrogating them. This is where the scholars disagree; are these rules considered to be a part of the Sharīʿah or not? For example, the verse that explains the rules of Qiṣaṣ (Retribution) in the legislation of the Jews. "And We ordained for them therein a life for a life, an eye for an eye, a nose for a nose, an ear for an ear, a tooth for a tooth, and for wounds is legal retribution. But whoever gives [up his right as] charity, it is an expiation for him. And whoever does not judge by what Allah has revealed - then it is those who are the wrongdoers."[94]

Another example from the same Sūrah is the verse, "Because of that, We decreed upon the Children of Israel that whoever kills a soul unless for a soul or for corruption [done] in the land - it is as if he had slain mankind entirely. And whoever saves one - it is as if he had saved mankind entirely. And our messengers had certainly come to them with clear proofs. Then indeed many of them, [even] after that, throughout the land, were transgressors."[95]

Both of these verses mention a law that was revealed to previous nations but they don't specify if they're applicable to Muslims or not. According to the majority of scholars these laws are also applicable to us as long as there's nothing in revealed texts that abrogate these ruling. Essentially, the real source of these rulings is the Quran and Sunnah itself.

93 Muslim, *k. al-masajid wa mawadi al-salah*, 521

94 5:45

95 5:32

13

QAWL AL-SAHABI: FATWA OF A COMPANION

A Companion is defined as anyone who met the Prophet ﷺ as a believer and died upon belief as well. There is unanimous agreement among the four Sunni schools of thought that the consensus (Ijmāʿ) of the Companions is a binding proof. As a matter of fact, it is the most authoritative form of Ijmāʿ. Similarly, there is unanimous agreement that the statement of a companion regarding those issues that aren't open to analogy or ijtihād are binding as well. For example, rulings that are related to quantities, numbers and time periods such as: quantities for zakāh, amount of mahr, minimum and maximum duration of menstrual cycle, and the maximum duration of post-natal bleeding.

However, there is a discussion as to whether or not the fatwa of a single companion is recognized as a legal proof and if it should be given preference over Qiyās or the fatwa of later scholars. According to the vast majority of Ḥanafīs, Mālikīs, and Ḥanbalīs, the fatwa of a companion is a legal proof and it should be given precedence over Qiyās. Imām al-Sarakhsī wrote, "In regards to the opinion of a Companion there's a chance that it's based on a narration. It's apparent from their practice that if one of them possessed a text they would either narrate it or base their opinion on it. There's no doubt that the opinion in which there's a chance of transmission from the Prophet ﷺ is preferred over mere opinion. It's in this context that the preference of opinion of the Companion over opinion is analogous to the preference of a khabar wāḥid over Qiyās. Even if their view was based on Qiyās, their view is stronger than all who are not Companions. The reason is that they were witness to the practice of the Prophet ﷺ and they saw the events that were the cause of revelation."

The Companions of the Prophet ﷺ were the best of people to walk on the face of this earth after the Prophets and Messengers. Allah ﷻ says, "And the first forerunners [in the faith] among the Muhājirīn (migrators from Makkah to al-Madīnah) and the Anṣār (those native to al-Madīnah) and those who followed them with good conduct - Allah is pleased with them and they are pleased with Him. He has prepared Gardens graced with flowing streams for them, there to remain for ever.. That is the grandiose achievement."[96] Similarly, Allah ﷻ says, "You are the best community singled out for people: you order what is right, forbid what is wrong, and believe in Allah."[97] The Prophet ﷺ said, "The best of my followers (ummah) are those of my generation (the Companions). Then those that come after them, then those after them."[98]

خَيْرُ أُمَّتِي قَرْنِي ثُمَّ الَّذِينَ يَلُونَهُمْ ثُمَّ الَّذِينَ يَلُونَهُمْ. قَالَ عِمْرَانُ: فَلاَ أَدْرِي أَذَكَرَ بَعْدَ قَرْنِهِ قَرْنَيْنِ أَوْ ثَلاَثًا ثُمَّ إِنَّ بَعْدَكُمْ قَوْمًا

96 9:100

97 3:110

98 Bukhārī, *k. faḍā'il aṣḥāb al-nabī* ﷺ *b. faḍā'il aṣḥāb al-nabī*, 3650

14

SADD AL-DHARA'I:

BLOCKING THE MEANS

The word "dharāʿi" is the plural of the word "dharīʿah", which signifies the means to obtaining a certain end result. Literally, the means to an end. the word "sadd" means to block. So the term means blocking the means to an expected end.

In the context of Uṣūl, it refers to blocking the means to an impermissible end that will result in some type of evil or harm. Prohibiting something that could potentially lead to something ḥarām. The means, or certain factors leading to something ḥaram would become ḥaram itself. It generally applies when a lawful means could potentially lead to an unlawful end or when a lawful means that normally leads to a lawful end is used to reach an unlawful end.

For example, khalwah (being alone with a marriageable woman) is impermissible because it can potentially lead to unlawful relations. Similarly, anything that may lead to unlawful relations is also unlawful. This whole concept revolves around preventing evil before it actually happens.

PART 3:

RULES OF INTERPRETATION

In order for a jurist to derive law they must understand the language of the law as well as have a set methodology and guidelines for resolving conflicts. Without an understanding of the language and without a set methodology, the derivation of law in a systemized manner would be impossible. As a matter of fact, it would lead to absolute chaos with everyone interpreting the Quran and Sunnah according to their own preferences, understandings, ideologies, and philosophies.

To understand the texts of the Quran and Sunnah properly, a person has to be familiar with the rules of interpretation. These rules provide a set methodology for a jurist to interpret texts and derive laws from them. In order to interpret the Quran and Sunnah with the intention of deriving laws from the indications they provide, it is necessary for the jurist to understand the language of the Quran and Sunnah clearly. A jurist has to have a deep understanding of words, their different usages, connotations, and their precise meanings.

That is why the scholars of Uṣūl have developed different classifications of words, their usages, and how they convey several different shades of meaning. The rules that govern the origin of words, their usages, and classifications are primarily based on linguistic grounds.

The scholars of Uṣūl classify words and their usages into four categories:

1. The classification of words with respect to their scope; is the word specific or general, absolute or qualified, or is it a homonym.
2. The classification of words with respect to their usage; is the word being used in its primary, secondary, literal, or customary meaning.
3. The classification of words with respect to their clarity; are the words clear or unclear.
4. The classification of words with respect to different shades of meanings that can be derived from the text.

This section of the booklet will explore each of these classifications along with examples from the Quran and Sunnah.

15

THE CLASSIFICATION OF WORDS WITH RESPECT TO SCOPE

This classification basically explains the grammatical application of words to concepts; does a word convey only one meaning or more than one meaning. Is the word specific in its application or is it general and can the absolute application of a word to its meaning be qualified or limited. With respect to their scope and application words are divided into four types:

1. khāṣṣ
2. ʿāmm
3. mushtarak
4. muʾawwal

AL-KHASS

A specific word is a word that conveys a single meaning that applies to a limited number of subjects. It is a word that has one member (subject). For example, knowledge and ignorance.

A specific word may refer to a particular individual, species, or genus. For example, Zayd is a specific individual, domestic horse is a specific species, and equus[99] is a specific genus. As long as the word is referring to a single

99 Equus is a genus of mammals in the family Equidae, which includes horses, donkeys, and zebras.

subject, concept, or idea it is considered to be specific.

RULING

Words that are specific are definite in their application and are normally not open to interpretation. A word that is khāṣṣ is definitive with respect to its meaning. Legal rulings that are conveyed in specific words are definitive and it is mandatory to act upon them.

If a khabar al-wāḥid or Qiyās apparently contradict a ruling established from a specific text of the Quran, one of two things will be done:

1. reconcile the apparent contradiction without changing the ruling of the Quran and if that's not possible
2. act on the specific text of the Quran and leave the khabar al-wāḥid

Examples:

1. "Divorced women remain in waiting for three periods."[100]

وَالْمُطَلَّقَاتُ يَتَرَبَّصْنَ بِأَنفُسِهِنَّ ثَلَاثَةَ قُرُوءٍ

This verse is explaining the waiting period of a divorced woman. It is specifically talking about a woman whose marriage has been consummated, has regular menses, and is not pregnant. The example of the specific word in this verse is "three" (ثلاثة). It is a word that has a specific meaning; it applies to a specific number. It can't mean more, as in 3.5, and in can't mean anything less, as in 2.5. Three is three.

Now the problem that jurists face when interpreting this verse is that the word "قروء", which is the plural of "قرء", is a homonym. It can mean menstruation (ḥayḍ) and it can also mean the period of purity between two cycles (ṭuhr). So is the verse referring to three menstruation cycles or three cycles of purity?

Imām al-Shāfiʿī ﷺ interpres it to mean three cycles of purity based on a number of different secondary arguments. For example, he uses a linguistic and grammatical argument that involves the

100 2:228

rule of numbers in the Arabic Language. According to the rules of counting for the numbers 3-10, the gender of the number will be the opposite of the singular of the object being counted. In the verse the number is feminine, which means that the object being counted must be masculine, which is ṭuhr and not ḥayḍ. Therefore, the waiting period of a divorced woman is three cycles of purity.

Imām Abū Ḥanīfah ﷺ interprets the word "قروء" as three menstrual cycles because of the specific nature of the word "three". According to the Ḥanafīs, the problem with interpreting the word "قروء" as periods of purity is that it necessitates moving away from the specific meaning of the word "three". The argument goes that the "Sunnah"[101] way of divorcing one's wife is to issue the divorce during a period of purity in which there were no sexual relations. If the word "قروء" is interpreted to mean cycles of purity, then the woman would count the one in which the divorce took place, and two more, which is less than three.

By interpreting the word "قروء" as three menstrual cycles, it makes it possible to act on the specific meaning of three.

There are a number of different issues related to divorce that are affected by this one interpretive difference:

a. The ruling of taking the wife back (الرجعة) in the third menstrual cycle. According to the Ḥanafīs it's permissible because she's still in her waiting period. According to the Shāfiʿīs it's not permissible because the marriage is done.
b. Permissibility of the divorced woman marrying another man. According to the Ḥanafīs it's impermissible because she's still in her waiting period. According to the Shāfiʿīs it's permissible because the marriage is done.
c. The ruling regarding residence and maintenance. According to the Ḥanafīs the husband is still obligated to provide her residence and maintenance because she's in her waiting period. According to the Shāfiʿīs the husband is no longer obligated to do so because the marriage is done.

101 Sunnah here refers to how the Prophet Muḥammad ﷺ corrected Ibn ʿUmar ؓ when he divorced his wife in a non-ideal manner (while she was on her period), and then taught him the more balanced proper "legal or Sunnah" manner. See: Bukhārī, *k. al-ṭalāq b. man ṭallaq hal yūwājih al-rajul 'mra'tah bi al-ṭalāq*, 5258

d. The ruling of issuing another divorce. According to the Ḥanafīs it's valid because the woman is still in her waiting period. According to the Shāfiʿīs it doesn't count because the marriage is already done.

2. "We certainly know what We have made obligatory upon them concerning their wives."[102]

قَدْ عَلِمْنَا مَا فَرَضْنَا عَلَيْهِمْ فِي أَزْوَاجِهِمْ

This verse is referring to the amount of mahr that is to be given to a woman at the time of marriage. According to the Ḥanafīs the word (فرضنا) is specific, it means to determine (قدرنا). So the meaning of the verse is that Allah ﷻ has determined, has set, and has specified the minimum amount of mahr that has to be given. Since this word is specific it must be acted upon. The issue that arises is that the verse doesn't specify what exactly that minimum amount is. So the verse is mujmal (ambiguous) regarding the amount. The jurists then turn to the aḥadīth to find the amount, which is found in the statement of the Prophet ﷺ, "There's no mahr less than ten dirhams."[103]

لا مهر أقل من عشرة دراهم

The Shāfiʿīs on the other hand consider the nikāḥ to be like any other financial transaction. According to them the amount of mahr is left up to the mutual agreement of the spouses, just like in any other financial transaction. According to the Ḥanafīs, leaving the amount of mahr up to the mutual agreement of the spouses necessitates ignoring the specific meaning of the word (فرضنا).

The specific word (khāṣṣ) can be further classified into muṭlaq and muqayyad.

---

102 33:50

103 al-Bayhaqī, *al-Sunan al-Kubrā*, 7:240

AL-MUTLAQ (المطلق): THE ABSOLUTE

Al-Muṭlaq is a specific word that is left unspecified in its application. Meaning, it is not limited or restricted by a description. For example the word "raqabah" (slave) in the verse that describes the expiation for breaking one's oath; Allah ﷻ says, "Allah will not hold you accountable for useless phrases in your oaths, but He will take you to task for the oaths you have made binding upon yourself. Its expiation for breaking an oath is to feed ten poor people with food equivalent to what you would normally give your own families, or to clothe them, or to set free a "raqabah" slave; if a person cannot find the means, he should fast for three days."[104]

فَكَفَّارَتُهُ إِطْعَامُ عَشَرَةِ مَسَاكِينَ مِنْ أَوْسَطِ مَا تُطْعِمُونَ أَهْلِيكُمْ
أَوْ كِسْوَتُهُمْ أَوْ تَحْرِيرُ رَقَبَةٍ ۖ فَمَن لَّمْ يَجِدْ فَصِيَامُ ثَلَاثَةِ أَيَّامٍ ۚ

The word "raqabah" in this verse is muṭlaq; it's absolute. It has not been limited to a male or female, believer or non-believer. As expiation, a person may set any type of slave they want free.

AL-MUQAYYAD (المقيد): THE QUALIFIED

Al-Muqayyad is a specific word that has been qualified or limited by another word such as a description or an adjective. For example, "raqabah mu'minah" in the verse that describes the expiation for accidental homicide; Allah ﷻ says, "Never should a believer kill another believer, except by mistake. If anyone kills a believer by mistake he must free one Muslim slave and pay compensation to the victim's relatives, unless they charitably forgo it;"[105]

وَمَا كَانَ لِمُؤْمِنٍ أَن يَقْتُلَ مُؤْمِنًا إِلَّا خَطَأً ۚ وَمَن قَتَلَ مُؤْمِنًا خَطَأً
فَتَحْرِيرُ رَقَبَةٍ مُّؤْمِنَةٍ وَدِيَةٌ مُّسَلَّمَةٌ إِلَىٰ أَهْلِهِ إِلَّا أَن يَصَّدَّقُوا

104 5:89
105 4:92

In this verse the word “raqabah” has been made muqayyad by the description “mu’minah”. It has to be a believing slave.

RULING

The rule of interpretation regarding those words or rulings that are derived from absolute words of the Quran is that their application has to remain absolute. They can’t be limited by a khabar al-wāḥid or Qiyās. According to the Ḥanafīs, limiting the absolute of the Quran through a khabar al-wāḥid or Qiyās is a type of abrogation, and abrogation through weaker evidence isn’t allowed.

Examples:

1. The verse of wuḍū’: Allah ﷻ says, “Believers, when you are about to pray, wash your faces and your hands up to the elbows, wipe your heads, wash your feet up to the ankles.”[106]

يَا أَيُّهَا الَّذِينَ آمَنُوا إِذَا قُمْتُمْ إِلَى الصَّلَاةِ فَاغْسِلُوا وُجُوهَكُمْ
وَأَيْدِيَكُمْ إِلَى الْمَرَافِقِ وَامْسَحُوا بِرُءُوسِكُمْ وَأَرْجُلَكُمْ إِلَى
الْكَعْبَيْنِ

According to the Ḥanafīs the command to wash (فَاغْسِلُوا) and the command to wipe (امْسَحُوا) are specific words that are absolute. They have specific meanings and can’t be qualified by anything else. That is why the Ḥanafīs disagree with the Ḥanbalīs regarding the basmalah.[107] According to the Ḥanbalīs saying the basmalah before wuḍū’ is wājib based off the ḥadīth of the Prophet ﷺ, “There’s no wuḍū’ for one who doesn’t mention the name of Allah upon it.”[108]

لا وضوء لمن لم يذكر اسم الله عليه

According to the Ḥanafīs making the tasmiyah wājib is limiting

---

106 5:6

107 “Basmalah” and “Tasmiyah” refer to saying the phrase: *b-ism Allāh al-Raḥmān al-Raḥīm*.

108 Tirmidhī, *k. al-Ṭahārah ʿan Rasulillah* ﷺ, *b. mā jā’a fī al-tasmiyyah ʿinda al-wuḍū’*, 25

the absolute nature of the command found in the verse and that's not allowed with a khabar al-wāḥid because that's considered to be a type of abrogation. The Ḥanafīs argue that whatever is established through the Quran is farḍ and whatever is established through the ḥadīth is sunnah. The same argument and difference in interpretation exists in the issue of sequence and intention in wuḍū'.

2. "Believers, bow down, prostrate yourselves, worship your Lord, and do good so that you may succeed."[109]

يَا أَيُّهَا الَّذِينَ آمَنُوا ارْكَعُوا وَاسْجُدُوا وَاعْبُدُوا رَبَّكُمْ
وَافْعَلُوا الْخَيْرَ لَعَلَّكُمْ تُفْلِحُونَ

From this verse the jurists derive the obligation of rukūʿ and sujūd in prayer. All four schools of thought agree that both rukūʿ and sujūd are obligatory parts of prayer. According to Imām al-Shafiʿī ﷺ it's also farḍ to observe a state of serenity and calmness (taʿdīl al-arkān) in rukūʿ and sujūd as well before moving to the next position of prayer. This serenity and calmness is achieved by allowing the limbs to come to rest and their joints to relax. The reason why he says it's farḍ is because of the well-known ḥadīth of the Bedouin who prayed quickly and the Prophet ﷺ told him to pray again.

It is reported that a man entered the masjid while the Prophet ﷺ was sitting in one of the corners and prayed. After finishing his prayer he came to the Prophet ﷺ and said salām. The Prophet ﷺ returned his salām and then told him, "Stand and pray, for indeed you haven't prayed." The man returned and prayed the same way he prayed before. He came back to the Prophet ﷺ and he told him the same thing. This happened three times. After the third he said, "By the One who sent you with the truth. I don't know any better than this so teach me." The Prophet ﷺ said, "When you stand to pray recite the takbīr and then recite what you know from the Quran. Then bow and be at ease in your bowing. Then rise until you're standing upright, then prostrate until you're at ease in your prostration. Then sit at ease. Do that in your entire prayer."[110]

---

109 22:77

110 Bukhari, *k. al-adhan, b. wujub al-qirā'ah li al-imām wa al-ma'mūm fī al-ṣalawāt kullihā fī al-*

إِذَا قُمْتَ إِلَى الصَّلَاةِ فَكَبِّرْ ثُمَّ اقْرَأْ مَا تَيَسَّرَ مَعَكَ مِنَ الْقُرْآنِ
ثُمَّ ارْكَعْ حَتَّى تَطْمَئِنَّ رَاكِعًا ثُمَّ ارْفَعْ حَتَّى تَعْتَدِلَ قَائِمًا ثُمَّ
اسْجُدْ حَتَّى تَطْمَئِنَّ سَاجِدًا ثُمَّ ارْفَعْ حَتَّى تَطْمَئِنَّ جَالِسًا
وَافْعَلْ ذَلِكَ فِي صَلَاتِكَ كُلِّهَا

Based on this ḥadīth taʿdīl al-arkān is farḍ according to the Shāfiʿīs.

According to the Ḥanafīs making taʿdīl al-arkān farḍ in rukūʿ and sujūd is problematic because it's limiting the absolute command of the Quran. The Ḥanafīs give consideration to the status of both evidences and say what has been established through the Quran is farḍ and what has been established through the ḥadīth is wājib.[111]

3. "And perform ṭawāf around the Ancient House."[112]

وَلْيَطَّوَّفُوا بِالْبَيْتِ الْعَتِيقِ

In this verse Allah ﷻ commands the believers to perform ṭawāf around the kaʿbah. This (perform ṭawāf) is an absolute command that is expressed using a specific word that has a specific definition. So limiting it by a khabar al-wāḥid isn't allowed because it's considered to be a type of abrogation.

According to the Shāfiʿīs, ritual purity is a condition for the validity of ṭawāf; in order for ṭawāf to be valid a person has to be in the state of ritual purity. They base this off the ḥadīth of the Prophet ﷺ, "Ṭawāf around the house is like prayer."[113]

ḥaḍr wa al-safr wa mā yujhar fīhā wa mā yukhāfat, 757

111 Refer back to section 3.5 to review the concept of Wājib. However, this is all legal semantics. If one prays without stillness in each portion of prayer (taʿdīl al-arkān), even the Ḥanafīs would say that the prayer is invalid. If done by accident, it would require the prostration of forgetfulness (sajdah al-sahw), but if done purposefully, it would invalidate the prayer. Thus, in terms of actual day-to-day rulings, it's legally the same.

112 22:29

113 Tirmidhi, *k. al-hajj 'an Rasulillah, b. ma ja fi al-kalam fi al-tawaf*, 960

الطواف حول البيت مثل الصلاة

The Ḥanafīs find this problematic because it's limiting the absolute nature of the command found in the Quran, which is a type of abrogation. They act upon both by saying that the act of ṭawāf itself is farḍ and being in a state of ritual purity is wājib. If a person performs ṭawāf in a state of ritual impurity it's still valid but deficient. The way to make up for that deficiency is by offering a sacrifice.

AL-'AMM

A general word is one that conveys a single meaning that applies to many things, not limited in number, and includes everything to which it applies. For example the word "men", "insān", and "whoever". The word "insān" (human being) conveys a single meaning but it applies to every human being without any limitation. It has an unlimited number of members (subjects). Another example is the word "Muslimūn" (plural of Muslim). It conveys a single meaning but it applies to every Muslim without limitation. A word can be general by its form such as men, students, and judges, or by its meaning such as people and community.

RULING

According to the Ḥanafīs the application of a word that is ʿāmm to all that it includes is definitive. The reason is that the language of the law is usually general and if its application were to be limited to only a few of the subjects covered by its words without any reason or authority to warrant a limited application, the intention of the Lawgiver would be frustrated. For the Ḥanafīs the ʿāmm of the Quran is definitive and must be acted upon. A khabar al-wāḥid and Qiyās are speculative. A definitive proof can't be limited or specified by a speculative proof.

The rules of interpretation of a general word of the Quran are essentially the same for that of a word that is specific. They are both considered to be definitive and must be acted upon. If a khabar al-wāḥid or Qiyās apparently contradict it then: if it's possible to act upon both without changing the application of the wording of the Quran, then both will be given consideration. If not then the ruling of the Quran will be applied.

Example:

"So recite as much of the Quran from what is easy for you."[114]

فَاقْرَءُوا مَا تَيَسَّرَ مِنَ الْقُرْآنِ

All of the commentators agree that this verse is talking about prayer. This is the verse that's used to establish the obligatory nature of recitation in prayer. According to the Ḥanafīs recitation of the Quran in prayer is an obligation regardless of whether it's Sūrah al-Fātiḥah or something other than it. The verse uses the word "mā" (what) which is general. That means any amount of recitation would fulfill the obligation.

According to the Shāfiʿīs the recitation of Sūrah al-Fātiḥah is obligatory based off the ḥadīth of the Prophet ﷺ, "There's no prayer without Surah al-Fātiḥah."[115]

لاَ صَلاَةَ لِمَنْ لَمْ يَقْرَأْ بِفَاتِحَةِ الْكِتَابِ

According to the Ḥanafīs this is problematic because it's abrogating the general command established through the Quran and that's not allowed with a khabar al-wāḥid. They reconcile between both evidences by saying that recitation of any amount is farḍ and reciting Sūrah al-Fātiḥah specifically is wājib.[116]

AL-MUSHTARAK (المشترك): THE HOMONYM

A word that is mushtarak is a word that has more than one meaning. It's

114 73:20

115 Bukhārī, *k. al-adhān b. wujub al-qirā'ah li al-imām wa al-ma'mūm fī al-ṣalawāt kullihā fī al-ḥaḍr wa al-safr wa mā yujhar fīhā wa mā yukhāfat*, 756

116 Again, this is all legal semantics. If one does not recite al-Fātiḥah, even the Ḥanafīs would say that the prayer is invalid. If done by accident, it would require the prostration of forgetfulness (sajdah al-sahw), but if done purposefully, it would invalidate the prayer. Thus, in terms of actual day-to-day rulings, it's legally the same.

a word that was coined for multiple meanings, and at the time of coinage, had more than one meaning. For example, the different Arab tribes may have used the word to mean different things. Some used it for one meaning, others for the other. Sometimes a word may have acquired a metaphorical meaning that became literal over time. For example, the word ʿayn depending on the context can mean eye, spring, gold, sun, and spy. Similarly, the word qurʾ means ṭuhr or ḥayḍ. Another example is the word "jāriyah", which can mean a female slave or a ship. The word "mushtarī" means buyer and it's the name of the planet Jupiter.

When a word that is mushtarak is used in the Quran or ḥadīth, it can only refer to one of the possible meanings. The Lawgiver — Allah ﷻ or the Prophet ﷺ — don't intend more than one meaning for a word at any given time. The rule with respect to commands and prohibitions is that the Lawgiver doesn't intend to uphold more than one of the different meanings of a homonym at any given time. It can't convey both meanings at the same time; one of its meanings must be identified. It would not be feasible to say "go to the ʿayn" and intend both a spring and the sun. Identifying which meaning is intended in the verse or the ḥadīth is the job of the mujtahid.

If a word that is mushtarak is found in a text, a verse of the Quran or a ḥadīth, then the mujtahid has to identify which meaning is intended. They will look at the context of the word, and how and why it is being used to determine the intended meaning. Once they have identified the intended meaning it must be acted upon.

AL-MU'AWWAL (المُؤَوَّل): **UNDERSTOOD MEANING**

After the intended meaning of the word has been identified based on evidence it's called mu'awwal.

Examples:

When a word has two meanings, one literal and the other technical (legal), and it occurs in a legal context, then as a general rule the legal meaning will be given preference. For example, the words ṣalāh, zakāh, ṣawm, ḥajj, and ṭalāq all have both literal and legal meanings. If they occur in a legal context then obviously the legal meaning will be taken unless there's some type of proof indicating otherwise.

1. "Surely, Allah and His angels send blessings to the Prophet. Believers, pray to Allah to bless him, and send your salām (prayers for protection) to him in abundance."[117]

إِنَّ اللَّهَ وَمَلَائِكَتَهُ يُصَلُّونَ عَلَى النَّبِيِّ ۚ يَا أَيُّهَا الَّذِينَ آمَنُوا صَلُّوا عَلَيْهِ وَسَلِّمُوا تَسْلِيمًا

The linguistic meaning of the word ṣalāh is supplication and prayer. Its legal meaning is the ritual prayer of al-ṣalāh: a set of specific actions that starts with takbīr and end with taslīm. Here the context tells us that the linguistic meaning is intended.

2. "Divorced women remain in waiting for three periods."[118]

وَالْمُطَلَّقَاتُ يَتَرَبَّصْنَ بِأَنفُسِهِنَّ ثَلَاثَةَ قُرُوءٍ

This is an example that was discussed earlier when talking about al-khāṣṣ. The word "قروء", which is the plural of "قرء", is a homonym. It can mean menstruation (ḥayḍ) and it can also mean the period of purity between two cycles (ṭuhr). Based on different evidences the Ḥanafīs interpret it to mean ḥayḍ and the Shāfiʿīs interpret it to mean ṭuhr.

3. Imam Abū Ḥanīfah ﵀ mentioned that if a man said to his wife, "You are like my mother to me" then he would not be a muẓāhir. Ẓihār in English is translated as injurious comparison or incestuous assimilation. Ẓihār is a type of divorce which was common in pre-Islamic Arabia, but was made unlawful by Islam.[119] It was a way for the husband to divorce his wife by selfishly saying to her, "You are like my mother." This way she would not have conjugal rights, but at the same time she would still be bound to him like a slave. The

117 33:56

118 2:228

119 See Sūrah al-Mujādilah (58)

reason why the above statement wouldn't be considered ẓihār is because the expression is mushtarak; "like my mother" could be a term of respect or it could mean you're impermissible for me like my mother. It will only count as ẓihār if he the husband had the intention.

4. "Believers, do not kill game when you are in Iḥrām.[120] If someone from among you kills it deliberately, then compensation (will be required) from cattle "mithl" equal to what one has killed, according to the judgement of two just men from among you, as an offering due to reach the Kaʿbah, or an expiation[121]."[122]

يَا أَيُّهَا الَّذِينَ آمَنُوا لَا تَقْتُلُوا الصَّيْدَ وَأَنتُمْ حُرُمٌ ۚ وَمَن قَتَلَهُ مِنكُم مُّتَعَمِّدًا فَجَزَاءٌ مِّثْلُ مَا قَتَلَ مِنَ النَّعَمِ يَحْكُمُ بِهِ ذَوَا عَدْلٍ مِّنكُمْ هَدْيًا بَالِغَ الْكَعْبَةِ أَوْ كَفَّارَةٌ

This particular verse is talking about the penalty of killing game while in the state of iḥrām. The issue that arises in this verse is that the word "mithl" (equal or similar) is mushtarak:

a. it can mean a similar animal
b. or the monetary equivalent

According to the Ḥanafīs what is meant here is the monetary equivalent. So the penalty is assessed by evaluating the monetary value of the game where it was killed. Then with that monetary value he has a choice:

a. purchase an animal to slaughter if it's equivalent
b. or purchase food equivalent to its value and give it as charity; each receiving ½ ṣāʿ of wheat or a ṣāʿ of dates/barely
c. or fast one day for every ½ ṣāʿ of wheat or one day for every ṣāʿ of barely.

---

120 State of consecration for Ḥajj or ʿUmrah.

121 Expiation, that is, to feed the poor, or its equal in fasts, so that he may taste the consequences of what he did.

122 5:95

5. "If he divorces her, she shall no longer remain lawful for him unless she "tankiḥ" marries (and consummates with) a man other than him."[123]

فَإِن طَلَّقَهَا فَلَا تَحِلُّ لَهُ مِن بَعْدُ حَتَّىٰ تَنكِحَ زَوْجًا غَيْرَهُ

The word "nikāḥ" is mushtarak between

a. marriage
b. intercourse

In this verse the Ḥanafīs interpret the word to mean intercourse. This is because the phrase "tankiḥa zawjan" is used. "Zawj" (spouse), would only make sense in the context of intercourse and consummation, and cannot be used to say "until she marries her husband". Either she's not married to him, so he is not her husband at the time, or he is her husband, in which case the marriage already took place.

123 2:230

16

THE CLASSIFICATION OF WORDS WITH RESPECT TO USAGE

The next broad classification of words is classifying them with respect to their usage; is the word being used in its primary, secondary, literal, or customary meaning. With respect to their usage, the scholars of Uṣūl divide words into four broad categories:

1. al-Ḥaqīqah (Literal)
2. al-Majāz (Metaphorical)
3. al-Ṣarīḥ (Plain)
4. al-Kināyah (Allusive)

AL-HAQIQAH (الحقيقة) AND AL-MAJAZ (المجاز): THE LITERAL AND THE METAPHORICAL

The literal meaning is defined as the original or primary meaning of a word. It's the original meaning that was assigned to the word when the language was being formulated. The metaphorical meaning is a secondary meaning of a word; when it's used in a way other than what it had been created for. For example, the word "asad". Literally it means lion. Metaphorically it can mean a courageous man.

When a word is applied literally it keeps its original meaning, but when it's used in its metaphorical sense, it's transferred from its original meaning to a secondary meaning. Usually, there's a relationship between the two meanings. There's a logical relationship between the two meanings and the nature of this relationship varies and extends over a wide range of possibilities. There are at least 30-40 variations of how the metaphorical meaning of a word is related to its literal meaning. Both the literal and the metaphorical meanings of a word can't be assigned at the same time.

Both literal and metaphorical meanings are used in the Quran. For example, Allah ﷻ says, "And do not kill the soul which Allah has forbidden, except by right."[124] The word "la taqtulū" carries its literal meaning. In another place Allah ﷻ says, "And sends down to you from the sky, provision."[125] The word "provision" is being used in its metaphorical sense, which means rain that leads to the production of food.

Words are normally used in their literal sense and in the language of the law it's the literal meaning that is relied upon the most. However, if a word has both a literal and a metaphorical meaning and the metaphorical meaning is dominant, it will most likely be used. For example, the word ṭalāq literally means to release or removal of a restriction from a tie of marriage, slavery, or ownership. Since the legal meaning of ṭalāq, which is divorce (dissolution of marriage) has become dominant, this meaning will likely prevail unless there's some evidence to suggest otherwise. Basically, the literal or dominant meaning will always be understood unless there's evidence suggesting otherwise.

Examples:

1. "But if you are ill or on a journey or one of you comes from the place of relieving himself or you have contacted women and do not find water, then seek clean earth and wipe over your faces and hands with it."[126]

وَإِن كُنتُم مَّرْضَىٰ أَوْ عَلَىٰ سَفَرٍ أَوْ جَاءَ أَحَدٌ مِّنكُم مِّنَ
الْغَائِطِ أَوْ لَامَسْتُمُ النِّسَاءَ فَلَمْ تَجِدُوا مَاءً فَتَيَمَّمُوا صَعِيدًا

124 17:33
125 40:13
126 5:6

طَيِّبًا فَامْسَحُوا بِوُجُوهِكُمْ وَأَيْدِيكُم مِّنْهُ

The verb "lāmasa" literally means to touch and has also been used metaphorically to refer to intercourse. The Ḥanafīs take the metaphorical meaning of intercourse; whereas, the Shāfiʿīs take the literal meaning of touching. One of the reasons why the Ḥanafīs interpret the word according to its metaphorical meaning is because of the narration that the Prophet ﷺ used to kiss his wives and then go lead ṣalāh.

2. Another example is mentioned by Imām Muḥammad in his famous book of fiqh *al-Siyar al-Kabīr*. He writes, "If a person requests amnesty in a state of war for his parents then the literal meaning will be understood and only his immediate parents will be included in the amnesty. His grandparents will not be included." The word "Ābā'a" has a literal meaning of immediate parents and a metaphorical meaning of grandparents. In this context, the literal meaning will be understood.
3. Another similar example is if a person requests amnesty for their mother, then only the immediate mother would be included in the amnesty and not the grandmother.
4. If a person takes an oath that I will never set foot in so and so's house, the oath will break regardless of how they enter the house. The literal meaning is to set foot but the metaphorical meaning, which is more common, is to enter in any way or form.

AL-SARIH (الصريح) AND AL-KINAYAH (الكناية): **THE PLAIN AND THE ALLUSIVE**

These terms are also translated as the Clear and the Implicit.

AL-ṢARĪḤ

A word is considered to be plain (clear) if it's intended meaning is absolutely clear. The word clearly indicates the speaker's intention. The word is clear, its meaning is apparent, and the speaker's intention is understood. For example, the words "I sold (بعت)" and "I purchased (اشتريت)". The interpretive rule of a word that is ṣarīḥ is that the apparent intended meaning will be understood. It doesn't require a specific intention from the speaker because the word itself is absolutely clear. In simpler words, when speech consists of plain words the intention of the speaker is understood from the words themselves and there's no room or need to determine the speaker's intention.

Examples:

1. For example, if a man says to his wife, "أنت طالق (You are divorced)", or "طلقتك (I have divorced you", or "يا طالق (O divorcee!)", the divorce will take place regardless of the speaker's intention.
2. "But if you are ill or on a journey or one of you comes from the place of relieving himself or you have contacted women and do not find water, then seek clean earth and wipe over your faces and hands with it. Allah does not intend to make difficulty for you, but He intends to purify you and complete His favor upon you that you may be grateful."[127]

وَإِن كُنتُم مَّرْضَىٰٓ أَوْ عَلَىٰ سَفَرٍ أَوْ جَآءَ أَحَدٌ مِّنكُم مِّنَ
الْغَآئِطِ أَوْ لَٰمَسْتُمُ النِّسَآءَ فَلَمْ تَجِدُوا مَآءً فَتَيَمَّمُوا صَعِيدًا
طَيِّبًا فَامْسَحُوا بِوُجُوهِكُمْ وَأَيْدِيكُم مِّنْهُ ۚ مَا يُرِيدُ اللَّهُ
لِيَجْعَلَ عَلَيْكُم مِّنْ حَرَجٍ وَلَٰكِن يُرِيدُ لِيُطَهِّرَكُمْ وَلِيُتِمَّ
نِعْمَتَهُۥ عَلَيْكُمْ لَعَلَّكُمْ تَشْكُرُونَ

According to the Ḥanafīs tayammum is considered to be a complete act of purification just like wuḍū' and ghusl. It's considered to be a complete replacement of wuḍū' or ghusl in the absence of water or the inability to use water. This is based off the words of Allah ﷻ, "But He intends to purify you." This expression is plain and clear because the word "تطهير" means the removal of impurity and the establishment of purity. This verse clarifies that tayammum purifies a person from impurities just like wuḍū' and ghusl. That's why according to the Ḥanafīs a person is allowed to pray whatever

127 5:6

prayer he wants, regardless of whether it's obligatory or voluntary, after performing tayammum.

According to the Shāfiʿīs tayammum is not a complete form of purity. Rather it's a way to attain purity out of necessity. Meaning, tayammum has been legislated, it's allowed, because of a necessity. That necessity is only for one prayer and the voluntary prayers associated with it. The tayammum will have to be repeated for each obligatory prayer.

Based on this slight interpretive difference a number of different issues are affected:

a. According to the Ḥanafīs it's permissible to perform tayammum before the time of the prayer. According to the Shāfiʿīs it's not.
b. According to the Ḥanafīs a person can perform as many prayers as they want with one tayammum. According to the Shāfiʿīs they have to perform tayammum for each prayer.
c. According to the Ḥanafīs a person who performed tayammum can lead those who performed wuḍūʾ. According to the Shāfiʿʿīs he can't.

AL-KINĀYAH

A word is considered to be allusive if its intended meaning is unclear and ambiguous. The word in and of itself doesn't clearly disclose the speaker's intention. The rule of interpretation for allusive speech is that the intention behind the speaker's words must be determined. This is usually done by looking at the context in which the words were spoken. There has to be some type of evidence or clues preset in order to determine the intention of the speaker. These clues can come from the speaker or from the circumstances in which the words were spoken.

Examples:

1. For example, if a man tells his wife, "أنت حرام (You are forbidden)" a divorce won't take place unless there's evidence to show that the man intended divorce. That's because the word "ḥarām" is ambiguous and unclear. It could mean "forbidden to me" or "forbidden to someone other than me" or "forbidden from doing something" or

"forbidden from leaving". Basically, it carries many possible meanings.

2. Similarly, if a man tells his wife "اعتدى (start counting)" it will only be considered to be a divorce if the man intended to divorce her by saying these words. The reason for this is because the word is allusive, it's unclear. It literally means to count or to take a record of numbers. It could mean count the blessings of Allah or anything else.

17

THE CLASSIFICATION OF WORDS WITH RESPECT TO CLARITY

The next broad classification of words is with respect to their clarity; are the words clear or unclear. Initially, words are divided into these two broad categories; clear and unclear. A clear word conveys a concept that is understood without recourse to interpretation. A ruling that is communicated in clear words constitutes the basis of obligation, without any recourse to interpretation. On the other hand, a word that's unclear conveys a meaning that's ambiguous or incomplete and requires clarification. These are words that don't convey a clear meaning without the aid of additional evidence that maybe given by the Lawgiver, or by the mujtahid. An unclear or ambiguous text can't be the basis of action.

From the perspective of clarity and conceptual strength, clear words are divided into four categories starting with the least clear:

1. al-Ẓāhir (Manifest)
2. al-Naṣṣ (Explicit)
3. al-Mufassar (Unequivocal)
4. and al-Muḥkam (Perspicuous)

These are different degrees or shades of clarity that words can convey conceptually.

From the perspective of the degree of ambiguity, unclear words are also divided into four types starting with the least ambiguous:

1. al-Khafī (Obscure)
2. al-Mushkil (Difficult)
3. al-Mujmal (Ambivalent)
4. al-Mutashābih (Intricate)

AL-ZAHIR (الظاهر) AND AL-NASS (النص): **THE MANIFEST AND THE EXPLICIT**

Al-Ẓāhir (الظاهر) is defined as a word or words that convey a clear meaning but this meaning is not the principal theme of the text in which they appear. As soon as a person hears or reads these words their meanings are understood; there's no need to think about what it means. It's a word or text that has a clear meaning but is open to interpretation.

Al-Naṣṣ (النص) is defined as a word or words that convey a clear meaning and this meaning is in harmony with the main theme of the context in which they appear.

The main difference between the two is that the ẓāhir doesn't constitute the main theme of the text whereas the naṣṣ does. This distinction seems very conceptual and theoretical, and it actually is, so perhaps a few examples will help clarify the concept.

Examples:

1. "Allah has permitted trade and has forbidden interest."[128]

وَأَحَلَّ اللَّهُ الْبَيْعَ وَحَرَّمَ الرِّبَا

In this verse Allah ﷻ says that he has made trade lawful and dealing with interest unlawful. The main theme of this verse is to differentiate between trade and interest. The non-believers used to say that there's no difference between trade and interest; they're both ways of making money. "They said trade is [just] like interest". Allah ﷻ responded by telling them that both of them are different.

128 2:275

This apparent and initial reading of the verse is considered to be the naṣṣ, or the explicit ruling of the text; that trade and interest are two different things.

At the same time, it is understood from the wording of this verse that trade is lawful and interest is unlawful. This is considered to be the ẓāhir or manifest ruling of this text.

2. "And if you fear that you will not deal justly with the orphan girls, then marry those that please you of [other] women, two or three or four."[129]

وَإِنْ خِفْتُمْ أَلَّا تُقْسِطُوا فِي الْيَتَامَىٰ فَانكِحُوا مَا طَابَ لَكُم
مِّنَ النِّسَاءِ مَثْنَىٰ وَثُلَاثَ وَرُبَاعَ

The principal theme of this verse is that polygamy is permissible and that it's limited to the maximum number of four. This is the explicit ruling or naṣṣ of this text that is understood initially from the apparent meanings conveyed by the words.

This text also establishes the legality of marriage between men and women, "marry those that please you." However, legalizing marriage isn't the principal purpose of the text. It's only a subsidiary point.

The effect of the ẓāhir and the naṣṣ is that their obvious meanings have to be followed and acting upon them is obligatory unless there's evidence to suggest a different interpretation. The rule developed by the scholars of Uṣū is that the obvious meanings of words should be accepted and followed unless there's a compelling reason to do otherwise.

What is meant by the ẓāhir being open to interpretation is that if it's general it can be specified, when it's absolute it can be qualified. If it has a literal meaning the metaphorical meaning can be understood. It also means that it could've been abrogated.

129 4:3

AL-MUFASSAR (المفسر) AND AL-MUHKAM (المحكم): **UNEQUIVOCAL AND PERSPICUOUS**

al-Muffassar is a word or a text whose meaning becomes completely clear through an explanation of the speaker himself. Since the meaning is absolutely clear through an explanation from the speaker the word or text is not open to interpretation or specification. The whole concept behind al-Muffassar is that the text explains itself. The Lawgiver has explained His own intentions with complete clarity so there's no possibility of interpretation.

This can happen in two ways; either the text itself is self-explanatory or the text is explained by another. For example, if a person says I owe you ten dollars it can refer to American dollars, Canadian dollars, or even Australian dollars. When the speaker clarifies and says I owe you ten American dollars it become muffassar.

Examples:

1. "So the angels prostrated - all of them entirely."[130]

   In this verse Allah ﷻ is telling us that the Angels prostrated to Adam ﷺ when He told them to do so. The word "Angels" is ẓāhir and its meaning is clear but there's the possibility of it being specified. Meaning some angels prostrated and other didn't. However, this possibility is removed by the statement of all "all of them entirely". So the text becomes muffassar or self-explained.

   al-Muḥkam is a word or text that is clear beyond a doubt and is not open to interpretation or abrogation.

2. "Believers, do not make fun of and mock (lā yaskhar) one another…"[131]

   In this verse is a clear and explicit command. The prohibition is clear, and is intended for that exact meaning: do not insult one another.

130 15:30

131 49:11

AL-KHAFI:
OBSCURE

Al-Khafī is defined as a word or text whose meaning is concealed and the intention is unclear because of a deficiency in the form in which the word is used. The meaning of the text is determined through further investigation. The ruling of a word or text that is khafī is the belief in the truth of the intended meaning and the obligation of investigating the intended meaning until it is elaborated.

An example of this is how the word thief is defined and understood in the Quran and Sunnah. The word sāriq is used, yet there is no set technical definition of the word. However, after analyzing all the texts regarding the rulings of a thief, it can be defined as someone who (1) takes an item above a certain value, (2) does so secretly, (3) and does so from a secure location. A person will be declared to be a sāriq if they meet these three conditions. That is why a pick pocketer who stole $10 would not fall under this category. Their actions still have legal ramifications, it can be called "petty theft", but it would not technically be considered "theft".

AL-MUSHKIL:
DIFFICULT

Al-Mushkil is defined as a word or text whose meaning is difficult to discover except by another evidence that removes the remaining ambiguity. It is considered to be the opposite of al-naṣṣ. The ruling of a word or text that is mushkil is belief in the truth of the intended meaning and the obligation to search for the meaning until such a meaning is elaborated.

The example here is the proceeding discussion regarding the waiting period after divorce. The word qurū' is mushkil and needs to be clarified.

AL-MUJMAL:
AMBIVALENT

Al-Mujmal is defined as a word or text whose meaning is not known except through some sort of explanation or clarification from the speaker. The ruling of a word or text that is mujmal is belief in the truth of the meaning and suspension of decision in it till the explanation or clarification.

Common examples of Mujmal are technical terms mentioned in the Quran without being defined in text, but rather through the Sunnah of the Prophet ﷺ. Whether it is the word ṣalāh or zakāh that appear all throughout the Quran, neither have set rules and guidelines presented within the Quranic text. Rather, the five daily prayers, their timings, their respective number of units have all been clarified by the Prophet ﷺ. And the same goes for zakāh: what percentage, how often, on what commodities, and so on; all of these guidelines have been set only through the Prophet ﷺ.

AL-MUTASHABIH: **INTRICATE**

al-Mutashābih is defined as a word or text whose meaning is completely unknown. There are no indicators, context clues, or narrations that help understand the intended meaning. The meanings of these words and phrases are known only to Allah. Due to the inability to understand the word or phrase, there is no legal ruling binding upon humans to act upon.

Common examples of Mutashābih are the *ḥurūf muqaṭṭaʿah* (disjointed letters) at the start of certain Quranic chapters. The letters and phrases like ***Alif Lām Mīm*** or ***Kāf Hā Yā ʿAyn Ṣād*** are things that are simply not understood by humans, even if some try and develop possible meanings. As a result, there is no action or ruling placed upon humans.

18

THE CLASSIFICATION OF WORDS WITH RESPECT TO DIFFERENT SHADES OF MEANINGS

One of the primary roles or tasks of a mujtahid is to derive law from the texts of the Quran and Sunnah; from verses of the Quran and aḥadīth of the Prophet ﷺ. A jurist will derive laws from a specific text after a very careful reading of the text itself that is grounded in the rules of the Arabic language. These rules guide a jurist's understanding of words, their meanings, usages, connotations, and how they may convey those meanings.

A text, through its words, conveys an obvious and apparent meaning. At the same time the text because of the way it is structured also conveys certain meanings that are implied or understood. The scholars of Uṣūl have categorized several different shades or levels of meaning that may be conveyed through a particular text. The Hanafīs identify four levels of meaning that follow a particular hierarchy beginning with the explicit meaning. The explicit meaning is followed by the 'alluded' meaning, which is followed by the 'inferred' meaning, and lastly the 'required'.

The explicit meaning ('ibārah al-naṣṣ) is the primary and principal meaning of the text. In addition to its obvious and explicit meaning, a text may convey a meaning that is alluded to by certain signs or indications within the words themselves. This secondary meaning is classified as ishārah al-naṣṣ, or the alluded meaning. A text may also convey a meaning that may not have necessarily been alluded to by the words themselves, but is related through the logical or legal implications of the text. This level or shade of meaning is referred to as dalālah al-naṣṣ, or the inferred meaning. The primary meaning is ʿibārah al-naṣṣ, the secondary meaning is ishārah al-naṣṣ, and the tertiary meaning is dalālah al-naṣṣ. This is followed by a level or shade of meaning referred to as iqtiḍā'a al-naṣṣ, or the required meaning. Without the required meaning the text would remain incomplete and not convey a complete or full meaning.

'IBARAH AL-NASS: **THE EXPLICIT MEANING**

The explicit meaning is the immediate meaning of the text derived from its obvious words. It represents the principal theme and purpose of the text. The Ḥanafī scholars of Uṣūl define it as the meaning "for which the statement was conveyed, and was intended purposefully."

هو ما سيق الكلام لأجله وأريد به قصدا

Examples:

1. Allah ﷻ says, "Do not take the life God has made sacred, except by right."[132] The apparent words of this text convey the ruling that homicide is prohibited. This prohibition is the primary meaning of the text, the principal theme, and the reason why it was conveyed.
2. Allah ﷻ says, "That is because they say, 'Trade is [just] like interest.' But Allah has permitted trade and has forbidden interest."[133] An initial reading of this text produces two meanings:
   a. trade is different than interest
   b. trade is permissible and interest is impermissible. Both of these meanings are understood from the words of the text itself and they are considered to be the primary meanings and principle theme of the text.

132 6:151
133 2:275

ISHARAH AL-NASS: **THE ALLUDED MEANING**

The alluded meaning of a text is also directly understood from the wording, but it is not the main theme of the text. It can be thought of as a secondary meaning that is understood along with the primary meaning. The Ḥanafī scholars of Uṣūl define it as the meaning "which is established from the sequence of the text without any addition. Neither is it apparent in every respect, nor was the statement conveyed for it."

ما ثبت بنظم النص من غير زيادة و هو غير ظاهر من كل وجه و
لا سيق الكلام لأجله

In order to explain this concept consider the example of a man looking at a person coming towards him from a distance. His main objective is to look at the person coming towards him, but at the same time he is able to see people to his left and right through his peripheral vision. The man coming towards him is similar to the ʿibārah al-naṣṣ and the people in his peripheral vision are similar to the ishārah al-naṣṣ.

Example:

> Allah ﷻ says, "You [believers] are permitted to lie with your wives during the night of the fast: they are [close] as garments to you, as you are to them."[134]

The apparent and obvious meanings of these words convey the ruling that it is permissible to have intimate relations with one's spouse throughout the entire night of Ramaḍān, from the moment the sun sets until right before the rising of the true dawn. This is the meaning that is understood from the ʿibārah al-nass. Through the ishārah al-naṣṣ jurists derive that a person can start their fast while in the state of major ritual impurity. This is a secondary meaning that is also understood from the text and is not the reason why this statement was conveyed.

---

134 2:187

DALALAH AL-NASS:
THE INFERRED MEANING

The inferred meaning is derived from the spirit and rationale of a legal text even if it is not directly conveyed through its wording. Unlike the explicit and alluded meanings, which are indicated through the words and signs of the text, the inferred meaning is instead derived through analogy and the identification of a common effective cause (ʿillah) between it and the explicit meaning.

Example:

Allah ﷻ says, "Say no word that shows impatience with them."[135]

The initial reading of this text conveys the prohibition of saying "uff" to one's parents. This initial and immediate understanding of the text is the ʿibārah al-naṣṣ. From this same text the jurists also infer that it is prohibited to say or do anything that would cause harm to one's parents.

The Quranic text on the expiation for erroneous homicide is used to illustrate a potential conflict between the alluded (ishārah) meaning and the inferred (dalālah) meaning. Allah ﷻ says, "The (expiation - kaffārah) of anyone who erroneously kills a believer is to set a Muslim slave free."[136] The explicit meaning of this verse is that erroneous homicide must be expiated by releasing a Muslim slave. By way of inference, it is further understood that freeing a Muslim slave would also be required in intentional homicide. The inferred meaning derived in this way is that the murderer is liable, at least, to the same expiation which is required in erroneous homicide. However, according to the next verse in the same passage, "Whoever deliberately kills a believer, his punishment will be permanent hellfire." The alluded (ishārah) meaning of this text is that freeing a slave is not required in intentional killing because murder is an unpardonable sin, and as such there is no room for expiation in cases of murder.

Thus, a conflict arises between this and the inferred (dalālah) meaning of

---

135 17:23

136 4:92

the first verse. The alluded meaning, which is that the murderer is not required to pay an expiation, takes priority over the inferred meaning that renders him liable to payment.[137] The Shafiʿīs are in disagreement with the Ḥanafīs on the priority of the alluded meaning over the inferred meaning. According to the Shafiʿīs, the inferred meaning takes priority. This is because the former is found in both the language and rationale of the text whereas the latter is not; that the alluded meaning is only derived from a sign. It is on the basis of this analysis that, in the foregoing example, the Shafiʿīs deem that the murderer is also required to pay the expiation.[138]

IQTIDA' AL-NASS:
THE REQUIRED MEANING

This is a meaning on which the text itself is silent and yet which must be read into it if it is to fulfill its proper objective.

Examples:

1. Allah ﷻ says concerning the prohibited degrees of relations in marriage, "(The following women) are unlawful for you: your mothers and your daughters . . ."[139] This text does not mention the word 'marriage', but even so it must be read into the text to complete its meaning.
2. The Prophet ﷺ says, "There is no fast (لَا صِيَامَ) for anyone who has not intended it from the night before."[140] The missing element could either be that the fasting is 'invalid' or that it is 'incomplete'. The Ḥanafīs have upheld the latter whereas the Shafiʿīs have read the former meaning into this ḥadīth.

137 Badran, *Usul*, p. 429
138 Abu Zahrah, *Usul*, p.115
139 4:23
140 Ibn Mājah, *Sunan, kitāb al-ṣiyām*, #1700

19

DIFFERENCES OF OPINION

Differences of opinion in Islamic matters are a reality. Anyone who's ever had a religious discussion is aware of that. Even a simple Google search can turn up a number of different opinions regarding a single matter. Oftentimes these differences can be very confusing.

A question that is commonly asked is that if all jurists refer to the same sacred texts, the same sources of the Quran and Sunnah for guidance, then why are there so many differences? In other words if all the scholars are using the same sources then why do differences of opinion exist? If the Imams of the four schools of thought derived all of their rulings from the Quran and Sunnah, then why have they differed in so many places? Another very important question is when is it acceptable for Muslims to differ over religious matters?

First and foremost differences of opinion in secondary religious matters have always existed. They existed amongst the Companions during the time of the Prophet ﷺ, they exist now, and they will exist until the end of times. For example, once the Prophet ﷺ told his Companions:

لاَ يُصَلِّيَنَّ أَحَدٌ الْعَصْرَ إِلاَّ فِي بَنِي قُرَيْظَةَ ". فَأَدْرَكَ بَعْضُهُمُ الْعَصْرَ
فِي الطَّرِيقِ فَقَالَ بَعْضُهُمْ لاَ نُصَلِّي حَتَّى نَأْتِيَهَا وَقَالَ بَعْضُهُمْ بَلْ

نُصَلِّ لَمْ يُرَدْ مِنَّا ذَلِكَ. فَذُكِرَ لِلنَّبِيِّ صلى الله عليه وسلم فَلَمْ
يُعَنِّفْ وَاحِدًا مِنْهُمْ

"Do not pray ʿasr prayer until you reach Banū Qurayẓah [a village near Madīnah]." A group of them were delayed on the way and the time for ʿasr prayer was almost finished. Some of them decided not to pray until they arrived, taking the Prophet's words literally. Others from the group insisted: "We will pray. The Prophet ﷺ didn't mean that we should skip the prayer." After they arrived, they informed the Prophet what had happened, and he didn't criticize either of them for what they did.[141]

Understanding when it's acceptable to have differences of opinion and the reasons behind them is extremely important because it provides a lot of clarity; it clears up a lot of misconceptions and misunderstandings. Understanding the reasons for differences of opinion amongst the scholars is extremely important in terms of both knowledge and practice.

In terms of knowledge, it's important because it shows the level of expertise and precision the scholars have in deriving rulings from the Quran and Sunnah. It shows how much effort they put into understanding the sources of religion. In terms of practice, it helps create a very high level of trust in their conclusions.

Having differences of opinion is not something that is negative or discouraged. Disagreeing doesn't mean there's conflict or opposition. This is something that is commonly misunderstood. Disagreement doesn't automatically equal conflict and opposition. That's why scholars usually differentiate between the words;

1. Ikhtilāf (difference)
2. Khilāf (opposition)

A great way to understand Ikhtilāf is that the goal is the same but the path to reaching it is different. When it comes to khilāf the goal and the path are both different.

The plurality of opinions within Islamic Law is a benefit and blessing for

141 Ṣaḥīḥ al-Bukhārī, *kitāb ṣalāh al-khawf bāb ṣalāh al-ṭālib wa al-maṭlūb rākiban w īmāʾan*, #946

the community, not a nuisance. There's a very rich tradition of diversity and disagreement within Islamic Law that has always been tolerated and accepted; **as long as that disagreement was valid**. This difference of opinion is something that is valid and allowed within the scope of the Sharīʿah.

The diversity of opinion that exists within Islamic Jurisprudence is an accepted reality and something that is actually celebrated. Imām al-Suyūṭī ﵀ said, "Know that the differences of the schools of thought in Islam are a big blessing and a great grace. It has a delicate (fine) secret that is understood by those who know, but the ignorant are blind to."

إعلم أن اختلاف المذاهب فى هذه الملة نعمة كبيرة و فضيلة
عظيمة و له سر لطيف أدركه العالمون و عمى عنه الجاهلون

One of those delicate (fine) secrets is that these differences allow the Sharīʿah to be flexible and adaptable. That's one of the features of the Sharīʿah that allows for it to be relevant more than 1400 years later. Another famous statement of the scholars is that "Their consensus is a binding proof and their differences are a vast mercy."

ISSUES THAT CAN BE DISAGREED UPON

Within Islamic Jurisprudence there are a number of issues in which there is a valid, accepted difference of opinion. There are also issues that don't allow for any difference whatsoever. It's important to understand that difference of opinion is valid only in those issues that allow for differences to exist. These issues are classified as mujtahad fīh, meaning a matter subject to interpretation. These are issues that are open to interpretation and allow for scholarly difference. A mujtahad fīh issue is any issue that does not have a definitive proof. Imām al-Ghazālī ﵀ defines it as, "every legal ruling that doesn't have a definitive proof".

Every legal ruling in Islam is based on some sort of dalīl, or textual proof; there has to be some basis for it in the Quran and Sunnah. That textual proof can either be definitive (qaṭʿī) or speculative (ẓannī). In order to determine what type of proof it is the scholars look at two aspects of the proof:

1. Authenticity
2. Meaning

Therefore, textual evidence is of four types:

1. Definitive in authenticity and meaning.

   When a text is definitive it's not subject to interpretation (*ijtihād*) so there can't be any difference of opinion. For example, the texts regarding the obligation of prayer are definitive. There can't be two opinions regarding the obligation of prayer, prohibition of alcohol/interest, oneness of God, or finality of the message of Muhammad ﷺ. There's a famous legal maxim: *There's no ijtihād in a matter wherein there is a definitive proof.*
2. Definitive in authenticity and speculative in meaning.

   An example of this is the issue case presented in the discussion about how long a woman needs to wait after being divorced (ʿiddah). The word used in the Quran is qurūʾ. The authenticity of the command is absolutely definitive; it is from the Quran. As for the meaning, it is a homonym, and thus becomes speculative in meaning. The Ḥanafīs say qurūʾ means three cycles of impurity (ḥayḍ), whereas the Shāfiʿīs say it means three cycles of purity (ṭuhr). It is understood from this discussion that the matter is mujtahad fīh, and is open to valid difference of opinion.
3. Speculative in authenticity and definitive in meaning.

   The Prophet ﷺ commanded that Sūrah al-Fātiḥah be recited in prayer. The meaning is absolutely definitive and clear cut. However, the area of difference arises from the level of authenticity. Yes, the ḥadīth is sound, but when looking at the mode of transmission, it is still a solitary narration (al-khabar al-wāḥid), and thus stands second to the Quran. As a result, the Ḥanafīs consider the recitation of al-Fātiḥah to be wājib, whereas the Shāfiʿīs consider it farḍ.
4. Speculative in authenticity and speculative in meaning.

   The Prophet ﷺ was asked if it is allowed to wipe one's leather socks (assuming the person who wore them already had wuḍūʾ before breaking it). He ﷺ responded saying, "yes." He ﷺ was asked, "Does it work for one day?" "Yes," he ﷺ replied. "Two?" "Yes," he

> ﷺ replied. "Three?" To which the Prophet ﷺ responded saying, "yes, and however long you need."[142] Now assuming this narration is reliable, the authenticity is still speculative because it is a solitary narration. In terms of meaning, it is speculative as well. The wording can be understood in one of two ways, (A) one can keep wiping on their leather socks for as long as they please without a time limit in which they have to remove them, make wuḍūʾ, and re-wear the leather socks. Or (B), the understanding of the vast majority of scholars, that the Prophet ﷺ was explaining that, as he ﷺ has clarified in narrations before, a resident can wipe over their socks for 24 hours, and a traveller for 72 hours. But this ruling isn't restricted to a certain time or place. If everyday someone was to make wuḍūʾ, wear their leather socks, and continue wiping for 24 hours after they broke their wuḍūʾ, that would be 100% valid. Even if they did that every day of their life. Not that a person can continue wiping on the same broken wuḍūʾ for more than 24 or 72 hours.

The last three categories (2-4) are all speculative proofs and thus subject to interpretation (*ijtihād*). For example, where to place the hands in prayer, how to determine the beginning of Ramadan, how many units of tarawih, the length of the beard, wearing pants below the ankles etc. Since they are open to interpretation there will obviously be differences of opinion. These differences of opinion can exist both within issues of Islamic Law as well as theology.

It must be noted that there are very specific qualifications for a mujtahid and the principles used to do so. As long as these differences of opinion are based on sound *ijtihād*, following the established rules of the Arabic Language and principles of fiqh, they will be valid. For example, according to the Shāfiʿī position a person should raise their hands to their shoulders when starting prayer. According to the Ḥanafī position a person should raise their hands to their ears. There are differences regarding how to hold one's hands in prayer, the ruling of reciting Sūrah al-Fātiḥah, reciting behind the Imām, saying āmīn out loud and the list can go on and on.

Issues of Islamic Jurisprudence aren't as black and white as people make

142 Abū Dāwūd, *Sunan, kitāb al-Ṭahārah bāb al-tawqīt fī al-masḥ*, #158 (There is some discussion about the authenticity of this narration.)

them out to be. As a matter of fact, they are very complex and require the expertise of scholars to comb through the Quran and Sunnah, search for relevant texts, then use the rules of the Arabic Language, principles of fiqh and their understanding to extrapolate and derive rulings. In addition to that they will look at the conclusions of previous scholars and experts and understand their arguments and reasoning for those particular conclusions. It's possible that two scholars will have the same verse in front of them but because of their different principles and methodologies will arrive at two opposite conclusions. Basically, fiqh is much more complex and nuanced than people think.

HOW TO DEAL WITH VALID DIFFERENCES OF OPINION

Adab al-Ikhtilāf, the manners or ethics of disagreement, is unfortunately something that is greatly lacking within communities. This is a subject that should be studied by all students of knowledge, Scholars, Imams, activists, callers, and the general public. How should these issues be approached and dealt with?

First and foremost, these issues should be discussed by those who have the proper qualifications to do so. Either students of knowledge or Scholars. Secondly, they should be dealt with a great level of tolerance and understanding. Just because someone follows a different opinion doesn't automatically make them wrong, lenient or somehow a deviant who's destroying the religion. There's supposed to be an attitude of acceptance and inclusiveness. No one should be rebuked, reprimanded, scolded, corrected, advised, or yelled at for following a **valid** difference of opinion. The Shāfiʿīs developed a beautiful saying, "Issues of *ijtihād* are not rejected with force, and it is not allowed for anyone to force people to follow their opinion regarding them. Rather they should discuss them using scholarly proofs. If one opinion appears correct to a person, he should follow it, and whoever follows the opposite opinion then there's no blame on him."[143]

Regarding issues of disagreement the approach and attitude of the Scholars of the past was always the following; "Our opinion is correct with the possibility of being wrong, while the others opinion is wrong with the

143 *Majmū' Al-Fatawa* (30: 79-80)

possibility of being right."[144] The reason for that is because there's no way to say with full certainty if a *mujtahid* is right or wrong. The mujtahid may be right and at the same time may be wrong. This is the attitude and approach that we should follow in dealing with differences.

The Companions of the Prophet ﷺ and scholars of the past had differences but they dealt with them with affection, love, humility, and most importantly respect. Although they disagreed they still had respect for the other person and their opinion. The scholarly tradition is full of examples of love and respect scholars showed for each other despite their differences.

Al-Imām al-Ḥāfiẓ Abū Mūsa Yūnus ibn ʿAbd al-ʿAlā ؒ said, "I haven't seen anyone more intelligent than Imām al-Shāfiʿī ؒ. One day I debated him regarding some issue and we went our separate ways. Later he met me, took my hand and said, "O Abū Mūsa! Isn't it that we can still be brothers even though we don't agree upon an issue?!"[145]

Similarly, Imām Aḥmed ibn Ḥanbal ؒ in praise of Isḥāq ibn Rāhawaih ؒ, Imām Abū Ḥanīfa's ؒ teacher, once said, "No one like Isḥāq has crossed the bridge to Khurāsān, even though he disagrees with us in many things. People will continue disagreeing with one another."[146]

One last example is that of Imām Mālik ؒ. Once Hārūn al-Rashīd told Imām Mālik that he wanted to make copies of his *Muwaṭṭa'* and distribute it across the Muslim world and make people follow it. Imām Mālik said, "O Leader of the Faithful. Indeed the difference of the scholars is a mercy from Allah on this nation. Everyone follows what is correct according to them, they're all upon guidance and they're all sincere to Allah."

The Muslim Community in America is very diverse. There are Muslims from all over the world who grew up learning and practicing opinions that may be different than ours. Children who are born and brought up here may even follow opinions different than those of their parents depending on who their teachers are. This is completely fine and should not be made into an issue. As a matter of fact when it comes to these types of issues people should be left to practice what they've learned as long as it's a valid opinion. Sufyān Al-Thawri ؒ said, "If you see someone doing something that's disagreed upon and you have another opinion, don't stop him."[147]

---

144 *Al-Durr Al-Mukhtar* (1: 33)
145 *Siyar 'Alam Al-Nubala* (10: 16)
146 *Siyar 'Alam Al-Nubala* (11: 371)
147 *Al-Faqih wa Al-Mutafaqqih* (2: 69)

This diversity of opinions shouldn't lead to disunity. Unity and conformity are two separate things. Islam requires unity, not conformity. This is seen in most major Masājid today where the Imām may follow certain opinions, some congregants may agree with him and others may not, but they still stand behind him in prayer. It's time for the community to mature and move above and beyond these debates.

FURTHER READING

ENGLISH WORKS

- Nyazee, Imran Ahsan Khan. *Islamic Jurisprudence: Usul al-Fiqh*. Islamabad, Pakistan: Center for Excellence in Research, 2016
- Kamali, Mohammad Hashim. *Principles of Islamic Jurisprudence*. USA: Islamic Texts Society, 2005
- al-Alwani, Taha Jabir. *Source Methodology in Islamic Jurisprudence*. USA: International Institute of Islamic Thought, 2003

ARABIC WORKS

- al-Shāshī, Niẓām al-Dīn. *Uṣūl al-Shāshī*. Beirut: Dār al-Gharb al-Islāmī, 2001
- al-Zuḥaylī, Wahbah. *al-Wajīz fī Uṣūl al-Fiqh*. Beirut: Dār al-Fikr, 1999
- al-Zuḥaylī, Wahbah. *Uṣūl al-Fiqh al-Islāmī*. Beirut: Dār al-Fikr, 1996
- Abū Zahrah, Muḥammad. *Uṣūl al-Fiqh*. Beirut: Dār al-Fikr

BIBLIOGRAPHY

- Al-Bukhārī, Muḥammad b. Ismā'īl. *Al-Jāmi' Al-Ṣaḥīḥ*. Cited by chapter, subchapter system.
- b. Al-Ḥajjāj, Muslim. *Ṣaḥīḥ Muslim*. Cited by chapter, subchapter system.
- Al-Nasā'ī, Ahmad b. Shu'ayb. *Sunan*. Cited by chapter, subchapter system.
- Al-Sijistāni, Abū Dāwūd. *Al-Sunan*. Cited by chapter, subchapter system.
- Al-Tirmidhī, Muḥammad b. 'Īsā. *Al-Jāmi'*. Cited by chapter, subchapter system.
- Al-Suyūṭī, Jalāl al-Dīn. *Al-Itqān fī 'ulūm al-Qur'ān*. Beirut: Al-Maktabah Al- 'Asriyyah, 2006
- Al-Haythami,
- Al-Hakim, Muḥammad b. 'Abdallah al-Naysāburi. *Al-Mustadrak 'ala al-Ṣaḥiḥayn*.
- al-Shshī, Niẓām al-Dīn. *Uṣūl al-Shāshī*. Beirut: Dār al-Gharb al-Islāmī, 2001
- al-Zuḥaylī, Wahbah. *al-Wajīz fī Uṣūl al-Fiqh*. Beirut: Dār al-Fikr, 1999
- al-Zuḥaylī, Wahbah. *Uṣūl al-Fiqh al-Islāmī*. Beirut: Dār al-Fikr, 1996

ABOUT THE AUTHOR

Shaykh Furhan Zubairi was born in 1983 in Indianapolis, IN. Shortly thereafter, he moved and spent most of his youth in Southern California, graduating from high school in Irvine in 2001. He began his pursuit of Islamic knowledge and spirituality at the Institute of Knowledge (IOK) in 1998 where he started the memorization of the Quran and studied the primary books in the Islamic sciences and Arabic language. After starting college, he took a break and went to Karachi, Pakistan for 9 months to complete the memorization of the Quran at Jamiʿah Binoria. He returned home and completed his B.S. in Biological Sciences from the University of California, Irvine in 2005. He then traveled to Egypt to further his studies of the Arabic language. Thereafter, his pursuit of Islamic knowledge led him back to Pakistan where he completed a formal 'Alamiyyah degree (Masters in Arabic and Islamic Studies) at the famous Jami'ah Darul-Uloom in Karachi, where he studied with prominent scholars. He has obtained numerous ijaazaat (traditional licenses) in the six authentic books of hadith Siha Sittah as well as the Muwattas of Imam Malik and Imam Muhammad and has also received certification in the field of Islamic Finance. Shaykh Furhan Zubairi serves as the Dean of the Seminary Program (IOKseminary.com) at the Institute of Knowledge in Diamond Bar, CA. He regularly delivers khutbahs and lectures at various Islamic Centers and events in Southern California.

The Institute of Knowledge Seminary Curriculum Series is a collection of books designed to build literacy amongst the Muslim community in the major branches of Islamic Studies including ʿAqīdah, Quran, Ḥadīth, Fiqh, Uṣūl al-Fiqh, Sīrah and Tazkiyah. The books go hand in hand with the with the courses offered through the IOK Seminary Program, which provides educational courses, programs and seminars to the wider local and international community.

Visit **IOKseminary.com** to learn more, view the full catalog and attend classes on-site, online and on-demand.

FORTHCOMING WORKS:

- A Brief Introduction to Tajwīd
- A Brief Commentary on Imām al-Nawawī's Forty Ḥadīth
- Tafsīr of Juz ʿAmma
- An Introduction to the Ḥanafī Madhab

NOTES

NOTES

NOTES

NOTES